WRESTLIN' JACOB

WRESTLIN' JACOB

A PORTRAIT OF RELIGION
IN THE OLD SOUTH

ERSKINE CLARKE

JOHN KNOX PRESS

Atlanta

To
E.L.C., M.D.C., L.C.

Library of Congress Cataloging in Publication Data

Clarke, Erskine, 1941–
  Wrestlin' Jacob : a portrait of religion in the Old South.

  Includes bibliographical references.
  1. Afro-American—Georgia—Liberty Co.—Religion. 2. Afro-Americans—
South Carolina—Charleston—Religion. 3. Liberty Co., Ga.—Church history. 4.
 Charleston, S.C.—Church history. 5. Slavery in the United States—Georgia—
Condition of slaves. 6. Slavery in the United States—South Carolina—Condition
of slaves. 7. Jones, Charles Colcock, 1804–1863. I. Title.
BR563.N4C57   277.58′733   78-52453
ISBN 0–8042–1088–8
ISBN 0–8042–1089–6 pbk.

Acknowledgment

Acknowledgment is made to the following for permission to quote from copyrighted material or from material in private collections:

To the Tulane University Library, Special Collections Division, for the selections from the Charles Colcock Jones Papers.

To Yale University Press, for quotations from Robert Manson Myers, ed., *The Children of Pride: A True Story of Georgia and the Civil War,* © 1947.

To Farrar, Straus & Giroux, Inc., for quotations from Lydia Parrish, *Slave Songs of the Georgia Sea Islands.* Copyright 1942 by Lydia Parrish. Renewed Copyright © 1967 by Maxfield Parrish, Jr.

To the South Carolina Historical Society for the document "Estate Sale! . . . by Louis D. DeSaussure . . .of A Prime Gang of 67 Negroes . . ." from the Major Hutson Lee collection.

Acknowledgment is made to the following for permission to print photographs:

To the John Huguley Co., Charleston, S.C., for photographs of St. Michael's Protestant Episcopal Church, Old Bethel Methodist Church, and the First Baptist Church of Charleston.

To the South Carolina Historical Society for photograph of Charleston, South Carolina, 1850, Smith and Hill, Delin.; Birds Eye View of Charleston, 1850, identifying the print.

To Houghton Mifflin Company for photographs of Miles Brewton's Slaves' Quarters and Servant's Houses, Anson Street, from Wooton and Stoney's *Charleston: Azaleas and Old Bricks,* © 1937.

To the Georgia Department of Archives and History for photographs of Negro cemetery, Liberty County, and Old Quarterman who was born a slave, Sea Island; from the Margaret Davis Cate Collection (from a copy, Ga. Department of Archives and History; original, Georgia Historical Society).

To the Collection of the Carolina Art Association, Gibbes Art Gallery, Charleston, S.C., for photograph of 39 Beufain St., Charleston.

PREFACE

The work on this book was begun with Eduard N. Loring and the idea of a joint authorship. His dissertation at Vanderbilt was on Charles Colcock Jones*, and we had hoped that he would write Part I on Liberty County and that I would write Part II on Charleston. The pressing demands, however, of his responsibilities in an intercity parish of Atlanta soon made it clear that he would be unable to participate in our original plan. In light of this, he very graciously turned over to me his work and research on Jones and gave me a free hand to use it as I would. This I have done, adding to it my own research—in particular, on the black slaves of Liberty County. The bulk of the Jones material in Part I, however, was provided by Dr. Loring, and I am deeply grateful for his generosity in allowing me to use the results of his labors. While Dr. Loring also read the manuscript—the section on Charleston as well as Liberty County—and made many helpful suggestions, the writing and conclusions are mine, and he bears

*Eduard N. Loring, "Charles C. Jones, Missionary to Plantation Slaves, 1831–1847" (Ph.D. diss., Vanderbilt University, 1976).

no responsibility for any of the flaws or errors.

Professor Justo Gonzalez, formerly of Emory University, read carefully and critically the entire manuscript. I am indebted to him for the contributions he made to the final shape of the volume. He is not, of course, responsible for anything in the book, but without his help there would have been many more errors.

I have received encouragement and help from a number of other people. Richard Ray of John Knox Press has given encouragement from the earliest discussions about the writing of the book. Joe Baggett's careful editing will be a benefit to every reader. Mildred Berry typed numerous drafts with skill and efficiency. J. Davison Philips, President of Columbia Theological Seminary, has been most supportive, especially during the final work on the manuscript. The Columbia Theological Seminary Library deserves special thanks for the help of Harold Prince, Professor of Bibliography, Lillian Taylor, Director of Library Operations, and Ann M. Taylor, Library Assistant. Dean Charles B. Cousar of Columbia Theological Seminary has been of particular help and support. His genuine interest in the work and his thoughtful ways of offering help deserve a special word of gratitude.

I am indebted to a number of libraries and historical societies for their many courtesies and the use of their collections. A particular obligation is owed to the church secretaries of Charleston who led me to records stored in old filing cabinets, vaults, and other obscure places.

No acknowledgements would be complete without expressing genuine thanks to my family for their patience and support during the writing of this book. My wife, Nancy Warren Clarke, and my daughters, Legare and Elizabeth, did not read the manuscript or type a single word. Nor did they simply bear with me—although they had plenty of that to do, and I am thankful for the grace with which they did it. What they did do, however, was to give me the gift of encouragement conveyed through their amazing vitality and their enthusiasm for their own work, interests, and play. And for that, I am most thankful.

O wrestlin' Jacob, Jacob, day's a-breakin';
I will not let thee go!
O wrestlin' Jacob, Jacob, day's a-breakin';
He will not let me go!
O, I hold my brudder wid a tremblin' hand;
I would not let him go!
I hold my sister wid a tremblin' hand;
I would not let her go!

O, Jacob do hang from a tremblin' limb,
He would not let him go!
O, Jacob do hang from a tremblin' limb,
De Lord will bless my soul.
O wrestlin' Jacob, Jacob, [etc., etc.]*

*"Slave Songs on a Mission," *Southern Christian Advocate*
[Charleston, S.C.], VII (December 29, 1843), p. 114.

CONTENTS

Introduction

A little over one hundred and thirty years ago among the low country plantations of Liberty County, Georgia, and along the cobblestone streets of Charleston, South Carolina, white preachers and black slaves were weaving a story that not only holds historical fascination but also insights for today. It is a story that is often surprising in its particulars, in the details that give flesh and blood, that paint a picture of southern scenes in startling black and white. And yet it is a story that also has meaning for those who seek to understand something of the human heart— the ironic pretensions that can blind the powerful, and the faith and courage that can emerge in the midst of suffering and sorrows.

Liberty County, Georgia, was the home of a remarkable community of Puritan settlers and black slaves. The Puritans produced patriots, planters, and preachers; the slaves, clinging with tenacity to a fragile African heritage, produced rice and cotton and a sea-island culture. In an extraordinary manner these Liberty County Puritans and Liberty County slaves encountered one another theologically. It was not, of course, a dry and abstract debate over obscure doctrines, but a struggle between owners and slaves, blacks and whites, over questions of life on a low country plantation. From this encounter the Puritans hoped to harvest not only good Christians but obedient and hard-working slaves, and the slaves sought not only to find hope for a better world in the future, but to forge resources for resistance in the present.

The focal point of this encounter was the missionary work of Charles Colcock Jones, Liberty County Puritan and "Apostle to the Negro Slaves." Nowhere else in the South was the "religious instruction" of plantation slaves undertaken with greater zeal or tenacity than in Liberty County. "In the county of Liberty, in Georgia," wrote the veteran traveler Frederick Law Olmstead, "a Presbyterian minister has been for many years employed exclusively in laboring for the moral enlightenment of the slaves. . . . I believe that in no other district has there been displayed a general and long-continued interest in the spiritual well-being of the Negroes."[1] Many agreed.

Jones was a wealthy and kind master, a dedicated Christian, who gave himself in the task of ministering to the slaves of Liberty County. From 1833 to 1847 he traveled from plantation to plantation and from preaching station to preaching station as a missionary for the Liberty County Association for the Religious Instruction of Negroes. A prodigious writer, he did more than any other person to convince the white South of its religious responsibilities to slaves—responsibilities that included not only the conversion of lost sinners to good and faithful servants, but also the provision for the physical needs of black brothers and sisters who were children of God. Jones' missionary labors in Liberty County provided, as perhaps nowhere else in the rural plantation South, the most intense encounter between a white preacher and black slaves. By looking carefully at this Liberty County story, a picture emerges of good intentions and vain illusions, of degradation, oppression, and the quest for dignity and freedom.

If Liberty County provides the clearest picture of the encounter between black slaves and a white preacher in a plantation setting, Charleston provides the clearest picture in a southern city. While there were many similarities between the plantation and the city, the urban context meant significant differences not only in the approach of white preachers and churches, but also in the manner in which black slaves were able to build resources to resist the oppressions of slavery.

Charleston claimed to be the "Capital of the South." It was a sophisticated and cosmopolitan city, proud of its past and careful of its honor. From 1830 to 1860 its pulpits were supplied by a number of distinguished ministers. They had been educated at Harvard, Princeton, and Yale, at the Universities of Edinburgh and Berlin. They traveled extensively in this country and abroad, carried on a voluminous correspondence with influential friends in America and Europe, and wrote scholarly books with such titles as *Apostolical Succession, The Unity of the Human Races,* and *The Vivaparous Quadrupeds of North America.* These ministers were clearly leaders of the church in the South and their names are still intimately associated with their various denominations. There was William Capers, one of the first bishops elected by the Methodist Episcopal Church, South, and the "Founder of Methodist Plantation Missions." There was John Bachman, distinguished naturalist and the founder of the Lutheran Synods in the South. Bishop John England was the preeminent leader of the American Catholic hierarchy and Thomas Smyth, John Adger, and John L. Girardeau were leaders among Presbyterians in the South and throughout the nation. In addition to these and other Charleston pastors, there were other leading ministers closely associated with the city: James H. Thornwell, "the Calhoun of the Southern Church," Bishops Gadsden and Elliott of the Episcopal Church, and Richard Fuller, probably the most outstanding of the Baptist ministers in South. No other city in the South or generation of southern ministers could match the distinctions or cosmopolitan perspectives of these Charleston pastors and their colleagues.

The black community in Charleston during this time was also one of the most important in the South. This was a community that had produced Denmark Vesey, the leader of an important but abortive insurrection in 1822, Morris Brown, one of the founders of the African Methodist Episcopal Church, and Daniel Payne, a leading black scholar who would become President of Wilberforce University and who with Morris Brown would have a black college named after him. This black community was one of contrasts: it had elite free blacks who owned substantial property and gained impressive wealth, and yet it was subject to one of the largest slave trades in the South; it had stability and a degree of freedom supplied by an urban context, but it also had the radical instability and cruel bondage revealed most clearly in its slave markets; it was faced with a profound racism on the part of the whites of the city, but it had, because of these racial assumptions and paternalistic attitudes, a generally relaxed and often close association with the whites. All in all, it was a black community well suited to deal with the challenge of white preachers in this "Capital of the South."

The encounter between the white preachers and black slaves of Charleston was the most important and interesting in the urban South. Because of the Denmark Vesey plot and its associations with an African Church, no independent black church was allowed in Charleston after 1822. While Richmond and Savannah and a few other southern cities permitted a limited number of independent black churches with their own black preachers, the authorities in Charleston insisted that blacks worship only under the supervision of whites. At the same time, however, white preachers in Charleston became very much interested in the religious instruction of blacks and gave themselves to this work to a degree that was unequaled in any other southern city. The results are surprising to later generations: large numbers of blacks and whites worshipped together, whites accepted blacks in ways that would be unheard of in a later segregated South, and blacks, almost unknown to whites, built defenses and found resources for resisting the degradation they found both without and within the churches of Charleston.

The white preachers of Liberty County and Charleston were

often kind and good men who sought to follow what they considered to be a moderate position. It was a position that has much appeal today to "political realists" who know the dangers of extremism and the need for prudent compromises. Yet moderation can have its own dangers, for these white preachers sought their moderate course within the confines of a cruel economic, social, and political system. What happened to them and the dangerous illusions that accompanied their efforts are not unimportant concerns for this last quarter of the twentieth century.

In the same way, the efforts of black slaves to both transcend and resist the oppression of slavery are hardly an irrelevant story for today. While that story is, of course, much wider than their relationship to white preachers and white churches, it has a particularly sharp focus in their struggle to deal with those whites who thought of themselves not as cruel and inhuman but as kind and good. The profound spiritual insights that blacks gained from this struggle and the resources they developed for their resistance can be an important gift to all today who struggle for dignity and freedom against those who consider themselves to be benevolent.

ONE

THE PLANTATION

1

The County
of Liberty

I

Two rivers flow through Liberty County, Georgia, marking its boundaries and telling of the land. To the north, closer to Savannah, the Medway rises and spreads its dark, cypress-stained waters into a wide, almost indolent, low country river. To the south, closer to Darien, the Newport in both its branches moves quickly and often treacherously between narrow banks until it too slows and spreads out and loses itself among tidal flats before emptying into St. Catherine's Sound. Both rivers flow out of the high sand hills of the piney woods. Here they are clean, fresh streams free of stagnant, mosquito-breeding pools; but as they move eastward, the tall pines on their banks give way to myrtle and oak and are swallowed up by cypress swamps where the wood duck nests and deer and turkey seek refuge. Spanish moss, the enchanter, the myth bearer, hangs from outstreached limbs while within its threads "chiggers" wait for anyone tempted to get too close.

At a point along both rivers, their character changes—they become tidal, their lower sections rising and falling according to the dictates of the moon; their waters, fresh at low tide, become brackish as the tide turns and pushes upstream against the river currents. Salt marshes begin to appear, filling the air with heavy perfume while bright-colored crabs and innumerable sea birds feed along rich mud banks, and an occasional porpoise moves through tidal creeks after mullet and shrimp.

Separating the rivers and the marsh from the open ocean are the sea islands. Colonel's Island, only three miles long, is surrounded by the marsh and tidal creeks, but stands high enough to overlook the mouth of the Medway. Between it and the ocean is St. Catherine's, one of the great sea-islands of the Georgia coast. Its broad white beach welcomes the sea turtles that lay their eggs in the warm sand and in its tall pines the osprey and southern bald eagle make their nests. Enormous sea-island oaks, gnarled and twisted, stand over dense thickets of yucca and myrtle, and palmettos run to the edge of the beach.

II

Into this rich coastal strip came Puritan settlers establishing a remarkable community. It seemed a strange place for Puritans— one usually thinks of them along New England's rocky shore or among snow covered valleys—but these Puritans had been wanderers, restlessly seeking the right place for their commonwealth. Their ancestors had left Dorchester, England, in 1630 for Massachusetts, settling there for five years before moving on to Connecticut where they had remained for sixty years. In 1695 a colony had left for South Carolina. There beneath the great oaks and beside the black waters of the Ashley River they had laid out their village and built their meetinghouse. As with most good Puritans, they had prospered—in spite of a sickly climate—so that within two generations there had been a need for new land. Commissioners were sent to Georgia and, after some negotiations, a grant of over 31,000 acres had been secured. In this way a colony of 350 whites accompanied by their 1,500 slaves began in 1752 a southward trek to what would become Liberty County.[1]

These wandering Puritans found the Georgia coast a good place to settle and to at last send down deep roots. The rich soil and the tidal rivers offered ample opportunity for the cultivation of rice and sea-island cotton. Yet as God-fearing Calvinists, they were aware of the seductions of such a rich wilderness, and they immediately set about establishing an organized community. They declared that they had a "greater regard to a compact Settlement and Religious Society than future temporal advantages." "We are sensible," they wrote in their Articles of Incorporation, "to the advantages of good order and social agreement, among any people, both for their Civil and Religious Benefit. . . ." They would not be lonely pioneers facing the wilderness on their own, but members of a well-ordered community. For these Puritan settlers, the government of such a community would consist of two coordinate branches: the Church and the Society. The Church would be governed by the male communing members who would administer spiritual affairs; the Society would be composed of all males who would subscribe to the Articles of Incorporation, whether they were communing members of the Church or not, and would administer temporal affairs. If this were not a "Holy Commonwealth," it was clearly a Christian Society they wished to establish on the Georgia coast—and, not incidently, it was just as clearly a society to be governed by white males.[2]

At the center of this community stood the church. Almost as soon as they arrived, the settlers built a meetinghouse in the most central location—halfway between Savannah and Darien. They named it Midway Congregational Church, although it was Presbyterian in everything but name (all but two of their ministers would be Presbyterians, and commissioners would be sent to Presbyterian courts). In 1792 a permanent church building was erected. It was a handsome meetinghouse with cypress siding. Two rows of windows, one high above the other, lined each side of the building to flood it with light and, in the spring and summer, with cool air. Inside, everything was orderly and harmonious. Straight-back pews ran in three sections across polished, heart-of-pine floors. At the end of each pew a small swinging door reminded all that these pews were rented, bought and sold, and were not available to just anyone seeking a place to sit. A graceful circular balcony supported by eight wooden columns supplied the seating for black slaves. Here there were long rows of open benches with only one raised board for a back. On the north side of the building a central pulpit was raised high off the floor so that even from the back of the balcony one could see at least the preacher's head. While the Baptists would later build one church at Sunbury and another by the waters of the Newport, and the Methodists would have a chapel not far away, this Midway Church was clearly the church of the district. For over a hundred years it would be a dominant influence in the community shaping its piety and perspective until Sherman's army shook the land.[3]

Close by the church, beneath great oaks with thick, heavy branches reaching down toward the ground, a cemetary was laid off and later surrounded by a high brick wall. Here during the coming generations, the community would bury its dead and record on stone monuments an astonishing record of achievement by the sons and daughters of Midway: two sons, Lyman Hall and Button Gwinnett, would be signers of the Declaration of Independence; and two, Daniel Stewart and James Scriven, generals in the American Revolution; four would be early governors of the state; one daughter of Midway would be the grandmother of Theodore Roosevelt, and one granddaughter would be the wife of Woodrow Wilson. Six Georgia counties would bear Midway names: Hall, Gwinnett, Stewart, Screven, Baker, and Bacon. One scientist, Louis LeConte, would be famous for his magnificent botanical garden growing in the rich Liberty County soil and be remembered for his two sons, John and Joseph, outstanding scientists and founding fathers of the University of California. Writing over two hundred years after the establishment of Midway, a distinguished historian would marvel at the achievements of this small community:

It would be impossible to name or even to number here the countless clergymen, doctors, lawyers, professors, teachers, scientists, judges, legislators, and soldiers who have left this tiny church to assume positions of influence and distinction throughout the nation and the world. For a rural community which at no time boasted more than a few hundred souls, and which was dispersed only a little more than a century after it was settled, such a record is indeed astonishing if not unique.[4]

III

This astonishing record was based not only upon the virtues of God-fearing Calvinists, but also upon the labors of black slaves. Over 1,500 had been brought from South Carolina with the first settlers. By 1845 Liberty County would have a population of 5,493 slaves, 24 free blacks, and 1,854 whites. The slaves who labored along the rice canals and in the cotton fields provided the economic base for the community, for from their toils and sorrows the whites would draw the necessary economic resources to establish their remarkable "County of Liberty."[5]

Of particular importance to both master and slave was the absence of owners from their plantations during a substantial part of the year. Swamps, marshes, and flooded rice fields made the region notorious for its deadly fevers. During the malarial season from May until autumn's first frost, many planters fled with their families to summer homes. Clustered in villages among the pine forests where the soil was sandy and dry, these summer homes provided not only an escape for the whites from the hazards of disease, but also an opportunity for a more active social life than the lonely plantations afforded.[6]

Because blacks outnumbered whites by almost three to one, and because whites were absent from the plantations during a substantial part of the year, there was less interaction in Liberty County between blacks and whites than in most parts of the South. For this reason slaves were slow to assimilate the whites' culture, and race relations were less intimate than in those areas where masters lived year around on their plantations. Freed from the constant presence and pressures of an overwhelming white culture, blacks in Liberty County, as in other coastal areas of Georgia and South Carolina, were able to maintain important links with their African heritage. Myths and traditions, voodoo and Geechee dialect, all pointed to the isolation of Liberty County blacks and to the tenacity of their fragile African legacy.

There were, for example, the "root doctors," powerful men and women who were both feared and respected for their secret knowledge of medicines and charms and conjures. And there were the drums that beat at funerals and dances, wood carvings that were clearly African in their beauty and design, and reed baskets and mats whose patterns reflected the art of Ashanti or Dahomey. And there were the Africans themselves, men and women who had been captured in Africa and smuggled in through islands and marshes long after the African slave trade had been outlawed. They remembered their homes, carried on their bodies the long or round marks of their tribes, and prayed at dawn with their heads bowed to the ground.[7] There was old Ben and Sally who would say when it thundered "maulin a bumba," and Golla Sylvie and Golla Tom, and the famous Belali Mohamet who was known up and down the coast for his Islamic faith and his efficiency as a slave driver on Thomas Spaulding's plantation. And there was Dublin Scribben who lived at Sunbury and taught his black neighbors an African dance song that would be remembered years later:

> Rockah mh moomba
> Cum bo-ba yonda
> Lil-aye tambe
> I rockah mh moomba
> (Cum) bo-ba yonda
> Lil-aye tambe
> Ashawilligo homasha banga
> L'ashawilligo homasha quank!
> Ashawilligo homasha banga
> L'ashawilligo homasha quank![8]

In spite of this isolation of blacks, there were important aspects of Liberty County that would lead white masters to that concern for the religious instruction of blacks that Olmsted praised so highly. Charles Colcock Jones listed six advantages in Liberty County for such a work. First, said Jones, the white population was noted for its "general piety and good order," and the people were ready to support movements for the public good. Second, the masters had the reputation of being "kind and liberal" toward their slaves, allowing them to hold plantation prayers, attend church, raise livestock and crops for themselves, trade at local stores, and visit in various parts of the county. While the community was not without its "severe masters," the discipline of the slaves was generally mild. Third, the whites felt at home here and shared a significant sense of place. Unlike many white Americans, they were, after they became established, "strangers to that restlessness, and indifference and negligence consequent upon the impression that they were settled but for a little while." Fourth, there was a strong sense of family among both the free and the slave that bound people together. "A result of this long settlement and association has been, that the white families and the Negroes with them, have become extensively connected by marriage and family ties, so that there is perhaps not another community of like size, in the world, in which there is a more perfect connection by family relations, in one form or another." Fifth, communications were easy. The plantations were not far apart, roads were good, and churches accessible. Finally, Liberty County was "far removed from the contaminating influence of any large town or city," and in 1829, with the beginning of the Temperance Reformation, the supply of alcohol had been restricted.[9]

Liberty County was, reflected Jones, "one of the *most favorable locations* for an attempt at the systematic instruction of the Negroes." Jones was no doubt correct. Religious instruction of slaves was most successful in the settled areas of the Old South where stability and order characterized community life. In a community such as Liberty County where both the black and white populations were relatively stable, it was possible to instruct slaves concerning their religious and moral lives with little disruption of the social and economic relationships between owner and owned.[10]

In listing Liberty County's advantages for the religious instruction of slaves, Jones failed to mention, no doubt from modesty, his own life and work among the coastal blacks. Yet without his tireless labors, there probably would have been little such work to excite the admiration of Olmsted and others.

IV

Charles Colcock Jones was eminently suited to be a white preacher to the plantation slaves of Liberty County. Born in 1804 on his father's plantation, Liberty Hall, he and his family were known and respected by the planters of the area.[11] Through a bewildering web of connections, he was related to many of the most prominent families of the community. Moreover, he was himself a wealthy planter coming to own, with his wife, three plantations: Arcadia which stretched from the Midway Church to McIntosh station and comprised 1,996 acres; Montevideo, a rice and sea-island cotton plantation of 941 acres whose plantation house overlooked the North Newport River and was the winter residence of the Jones' family; and Maybank, a 700 acre sea-island cotton plantation located on Colonel's Island where the Jones' summer retreat overlooked the mouth of the Medway River. To work these plantations and serve as family "servants," Jones owned over one hundred black slaves. With such family connections and planting interests, it is not surprising that the slaveholders of Liberty County regarded Jones as one of their own—and that would be a vital factor for the delicate task of providing Georgia slaves with religious instructions.[12]

Jones, however, was not simply Liberty County "born and bred." As a young man, he had followed the trail of his Puritan ancestors back to New England, back to Massachusetts, for a proper education. He had entered Phillips Academy, Andover, and two years later he had moved across the street to Andover Theological Seminary which had been established by Jedidiah Morse, a former pastor of Midway. This was the place, Jones was sure, for a proper theological education: there were no slow, cypress-stained rivers or balmy breezes carrying the taste of salt from the marsh, but cold winters that left the mind clear and sharp, and pure snow that called for the reformation of the heart. And, most important of all, there was no slavery. "Were you my dear," he wrote to his first cousin and fiancée Mary Jones, "to reside a few months only in a free community you would see more clearly than you now do the evil of slavery. There is a calmness, an order, a morality, a general sentiment of right and wrong which is not to be looked for in ours." Just the right atmosphere, he thought, for studying theology.[13]

But Andover was no bastion of liberalism. It was rather a protest against Harvard and its liberalism—the theological, not social variety—and had become a rallying point for orthodoxy. It had a brilliant and aggressive faculty including Leonard Woods, in whose home Jones was fortunate enough to find a room, and Ebenezer Porter, who became Jones' close friend and advisor. The student body was large and enthusiastic and carried the influence of the school throughout the country and into the growing mission fields abroad. These Andover student and faculty members were orthodox, but they were also reformers: zealous, committed reformers, who were, nevertheless, prudent and cautious, for their orthodoxy had taught them to treasure harmony, balance, and reason. And so they had formed great voluntary societies to accomplish benevolent ends. There had been the American Tract Society, the American Board of Commissioners for Foreign Missions, the American Home Missionary Society, the American Education Society, and the American Temperance Society—all non-denominational and voluntary, all powerful instruments of an aggressive American evangelicalism, and all intimately connected with Andover's students and faculty.[14] For the young seminary student from Liberty County, the structures and goals of these voluntary societies would become important sources for his work as a preacher to black slaves.

For his final year of theological education, Jones left Andover and entered Princeton Theological Seminary. Even then it was rather stodgy, more orthodox even than Andover and lacking its excitement. It was for Jones, however, a move south from Massachusetts toward home and reflected his growing concern over the question of slavery. For some time he had been struggling with this issue and an appropriate Christian response to it. At both Andover and Princeton he had found an atmosphere in which slavery was regarded as a great evil like war, but not a sin *per se* (the Bible would have to condemn it directly, so the argument went, for slaveholders to be sinners). The influence of the gospel, it was thought, was toward emancipation—but it was an evolutionary process and not a radical, imprudent abolitionism; and because of supposed racial differences, colonization was believed to be the best answer to slavery and the bright hope for the conversion of Africa. It was a compassionate and concerned approach, only most of its compassion and concern were directed toward southern slaveholders who had such a "heavy burden to bear" with this alien race.[15]

Still Jones agonized. There were no easy answers for him. "I have spent many an anxious thought upon the subject of slavery," he wrote his fiancée in Liberty County. "The more I look at it, the more enormous does it appear." Slavery, said the Georgia Puritan, is a "violation of all the laws of God and man at once. A complete annihilation of justice. An inhuman abuse of power, and an assumption of the responsibility of fixing the life and destiny of immortal beings, fearful in extreme." He caught glimpses of a handwriting on the wall and heard in the distance a firebell in the night. He wondered if God designed to overthrow southern slaveholding with a "tenfold vengeance" to be visited on "those who continue the wickedness," or if the "omnipotence of divine truth" would allow slavery to be removed in a peaceful manner. He hoped for the latter. He prayed for the latter. And he wondered about his own continuing personal involvement with the guilt of his land: "How often do I think of the number of hands employed to furnish me with those conveniences of life of which they are in consequence deprived—how many intellects, how many souls perhaps, withered and blasted forever for this very purpose! . . . What I would not give if our family were not freed of this property and removed beyond its influence!"[16]

What could he give, or rather what would he give, to be free from such a burden? How could he find a righteous path in the midst of the "wickedness" of slavery? How could he find innocence in the midst of so much guilt? For the young seminarian from Liberty County, there seemed to be no simple answers to these questions, but some alternate paths appeared to be opened to him. While still a student at Andover, he had at first turned to the American Colonization Society as the best hope for overcoming the evils. It seemed such a glorious scheme, full of reason and so lacking in pain. The black population of the country would simply be removed to West Africa where a "civilized and Christianized republic" could be established in Liberia. There, Jones had dreamed, the former slaves could form a powerful republic

> to suppress the slave trade on the western shore, and if possible on the eastern—to open extensive trade with the nations in the interior of Africa to send them teachers and missionaries to reclaim them from their heathenish condition. . . . What bright hopes of the suppression of the horrible traffic, the slave trade? What bright hopes of the ultimate destruction of the system of slavery? Of the rescue of nearly 3,000,000 of immortal beings from ignorance, oppression, and iniquity, their establishment as a free people among the nations of the earth, and the consequent happiness and usefulness to God and man, of that immense increase of population descending from them to the end of time? What a noble design![17]

It was noble indeed—unless, of course, you happened to be a black who did not want to be "removed," or a white planter who had no desire to lose valuable property and slave labor. Then you might consider it as less than noble and greet its proposal as impossibly naïve. And that is what happened. The Society with its implicit racism and its economic and political naiveté would soon be overwhelmed by the growing passions of the slavery controversy and lose its appeal.

Jones considered for a time an alternative path, a daring and radical path, that would have freed him from an immediate involvement as a slaveholder—the emancipation of his own slaves. He struggled with this question in a manner that was representative of those southern whites who felt the force of anti-slavery arguments:

> I am moreover undecided whether I ought to *hold slaves*. As to the *principle* of slavery, it is wrong! It is unjust and contrary to nature and religion to hold men enslaved. But the question is, in my present circumstances, with the evil of my hands entailed from my father, would the general interest of the slaves and community at large, with reference to the slaves themselves, be promoted best, by emancipation? Could I do more for the ultimate good of the slave population by holding or emancipating what I own?[18]

During his seminary career, this question was of utmost importance for the young Georgian. He had before him the example of his friend J. Leighton Wilson who had met the question squarely, freed over 30 slaves on his South Carolina plantation, paid for their transportation to Liberia, and helped to establish them there. But Jones could not bring himself to give this answer. As was true for most slaveholders who struggled with the question, his answer would be found in the events and economics of southern history and in the seductive power of southern society.[19]

Jones, however, was still faced with the question of what he was to do in the face of the "wickedness" of slavery. More and more he began to turn his face southward along a third path that led to Liberty County, where home and family, roots and traditions drew his troubled heart. More and more he began to see himself as a missionary to the slaves of Liberty County, as one who would pour out his life and energies laboring among those black men and women who were so much a part of his homeland.[20]

Jones was aware that such a missionary task would involve

great sensitivity toward the defensiveness of southern feelings. Writing from Princeton to Mary Jones, he noted that there "have been many ministers who have ruined their influence and usefulness in the southern states, by injudicious speech and conduct in regard to the slaves and the general subject of slavery." It is highly important, wrote Jones, that those who were "anticipating a Southern field of labour, should become well acquainted with the subject of slavery, and understand in what way it may be approached, and by what course of conduct the best interests of the coloured population and the approbation of the whites may be secured." Jones was expressing to his fiancée the great dilemma of any white who wished to labor as a missionary among black slaves. On the one hand, the "best interest of the coloured population" had to be understood and acted upon; on the other hand, the "approbation of the whites" must be secured. It was becoming increasingly clear, however, that the one criterion for the "approbation of the whites" was the support of slavery. This would mean for Jones, and for all others who wished to labor as missionaries among the slaves, that they must accommodate themselves to the stringent demands of southern society.[21]

V

Charles Colcock Jones came home to Liberty County in the fall of 1830. Within a month he would be married to his first cousin Mary, and within four months he would begin his labors as a missionary to the slaves of Liberty County. The decision to return to his southern home meant for Jones that the anti-slavery sentiment of his seminary days would be put behind him. (It would, after all, be awkward and impolite to express such feelings among family and friends.) For to come home to the South that he loved, to come home to his plantation and slaves, to the gracious and hospitable "County of Liberty," meant that in the end what he gave up was not his slaves but some of his own freedom and moral vision. Such was the path of the young seminarian. That he never saw the dangers, that he never questioned seeking righteousness and innocence by such a path, would become part of the profound irony of his life.

Jones soon established himself as the wealthy planter that he was. The home he built at Montevideo was perhaps typical of other plantations in the area. The house itself was not a pretentious "southern mansion" of the Greek Revival style with great columns and a wide veranda, it was no Barrington Hall that his young friend Barrington King would build at Roswell or Montrose that his own son Charles, Jr., would later buy at Augusta; nor was it a magnificent brick home of an earlier period that could be found along the rivers of Virginia and South Carolina, no Drayton Hall or Middleton Place. It was rather more of a country home, simple in its design and plain in its appearance. In the style of a Charleston singlehouse, it looked, for those who knew, much like ancient Middleburg Plantation not far from where Jones' ancestors had settled at Dorchester. Its very simplicity, however, gave it an aesthetic appeal, a quality of beauty, that came through its relationship to the land and its suggestions about the life of the people. It was a two-story house with seven windows across the front on the upper floor and six windows plus a door on the lower. Immediately beneath the second story windows a slated roof, supported by eight slender columns, extended out to cover a porch. It was here on this porch, late in the afternoons, that tea would be served to the family and their guests. From their seats a clear view of the North Newport River was possible, and the marsh grass could be seen waving green in the summer and brown in winter. "The house" wrote Mary Jones,

> is beautifully located, on one side fronting a lawn of twenty or thirty acres covered with live oaks, magnolias, cedars, pines, and many other forest trees, arranged in groves or stretching out in lines and avenues or dotting the lawn here and there. On the other front passes the North Newport River, where all the produce of the place may be shipped to Savannah and water communications

obtained to any point. In the gardens will be found both sweet and sour oranges, and the myrtle orange, pomegranates, figs, the bearing olive, and grapes. . . . Attached to the house lot are a brick kitchen, brick dairy, smoke-house, washing and weaving rooms, two servants' houses, a commodius new stable and a carriage house and wagon shed, various poultry houses and yards attached, a well of excellent water, and a never-failing spring. On the plantation settlement are a two-story cotton house, gin and gin house, barn, corn house, rice house, winnowing house, mill house, and fifteen frame houses, a brick shed and yard of excellent clay, and a chapel twenty by thirty feet.

Beyond his own economic involvement in slavery, beyond the pressures of southern society, it would have been difficult for Jones to give up such an enticing scene. For this was a picture that enchanted the southern imagination: a lovely, self-sufficient plantation high above a flowing river. Moral indignation about the evils of slavery would have little power over the seduction of such a southern home.[22]

Near the plantation house at Montevideo were "two servants' houses." It was here no doubt that the domestic slaves lived. Over the next thirty years these would include Mom Lucy and her husband Charles, Mom Patience and her husband Porter. There would be Phoebe and Clarissa the seamstresses, Marcia the cook, Gilbert the carriage driver, Jupiter and Caesar the gardeners, Niger the fisherman, and Cato the foreman. In addition, there were "sundry younger servants," who were "commissioned to sweep, scrub, brush flies, and run on errands."[23] The Jones' relationship with these domestic servants was kind and paternal: they were regarded as part of the household and were looked upon with genuine affection. (Mary Jones would be shocked and disillusioned when emancipation revealed resentment and a lack of loyalty among many family "servants.")[24] They were all slaves that Jones and his wife had inherited. Like most of the slaves of Liberty County, they had spent their lives, as had their parents and grandparents, in this land of high sand hills and flowing rivers, rice and cotton fields. Without being sentimental, one could say that they knew, in spite of their bondage and heavy

labors, the enchantment and beauty of this land. They too knew
the smell of the salty air and the way it felt blowing up from the
marsh onto their faces. They had roamed its woods and fished its
rivers and canals. They had looked out with pride on the dikes
they had built and the fields of cotton they had planted and had
called it theirs. "I have been for parts of two weeks on our
marsh," wrote Cato to Jones away in Philadelphia, "Stopping the
big cut which I am Satisfied is now Secure. . . . I think we will make
Thirty Bales [of cotton] unless I am much decieved. The cattepill-
ers are all over the country & as near us as Maj Porters, but not
in ours as yet. . . ."[25] It was "our" marsh and "our" cotton, and
they could be proud of it though they could never own it. As
much as for Jones, this place was home for them. They had
parents and grandparents here with aunts and uncles, cousins
and friends scattered throughout the country. In Jones' own
words, they were "extensively connected by marriage and family
ties." There was in fact a certain intensity in their identification
with this place, not in spite of their slavery, but precisely because
of it and its terrors. Frederick Douglass said it best:

> The people of the North, and free people generally, I think, have
> less attachment to the places where they are born and brought up
> than had the slaves. Their freedom to come and go, to be here and
> there, as they list, prevents any extravagant attachment to any one
> place. On the other hand, the slave was a fixture, he had no choice,
> no goal but was pegged down to one single spot, and must take
> root there or die. The idea of removal elsewhere came generally
> in the shape of a threat, and in punishment for crime. It was
> therefore attended with fear and dread. The enthusiasm which
> animates young freemen, when they contemplate a life in the far
> west, or in some distant country, where they expect to rise to
> wealth and distinction, could have no place in the thought of the
> slave; nor could those from whom they separated know anything
> of that cheerfulness with which friends and relations yield each
> other up, when they feel that it is for the good of the departing one
> that he is removed from his native place. Then, too, there is corre-
> spondence and the hope of reunion, but with the slaves, all these
> mitigating circumstances were wanting. There was no improve-
> ment in condition *probable*—no correspondence *possible*—no reun-

ion attainable. His going out into the fields was like a living man going into a tomb, who, with open eyes, sees himself buried out of sight and hearing of wife, children, and friends of kindred tie.[26]

While the Jones lived in close proximity to the domestic slaves, the very structure of the plantation allowed most blacks to be kept at a distance from the whites. Montevideo with its gardens, dairy, and smokehouse, its weaving rooms, gin, and chapel, was in many ways self-sufficient. For the fieldhands in particular, this meant that the plantation and the immediate area around it was an isolated world. Even on the plantation itself, most blacks were segregated from the white family and lived on the "plantation settlement" well beyond the "Big House." This arrangement, in addition to the relatively few whites and their absence during a substantial part of the year, left the blacks of Liberty County far removed from the influences of the white culture.

For Charles Jones this isolation of black slaves meant that they were a field for missionary endeavors. If he were not to pursue his anti-slavery sentiments, he could take another path, he could turn to these black people in the hope of bringing them the gospel and elevating their conditions in the midst of slavery. "What induced me in the beginning," he would later write, "to undertake the work of the religious instruction of the negroes was an interest in them as an ignorant, degraded, destitute, neglected and perishing people."[27] For almost fifteen years he would labor among these people. He would strive to make Liberty County a model for the South, an example of what could be done for the religious instruction of black slaves.

2

"They Lifted Up
Their Voices
and Wept"

I

What was needed, Jones now thought, was a cautious, prudent approach to this question of slavery. This was the only way that any real progress could be made, the only possible way that salvation could be brought to the blacks who labored in southern fields. Without caution there could be no preaching of the gospel; without moderation there could be no reforms within slavery. Jones knew the South too well; it was too much a part of his heart, too deeply ingrained in his manners for there to be any questions on this point—if he wanted to work in the South among the slaves, he had to use not only the wisdom of Solomon but all his knowledge of southern manners, all his family connections, and all of his prestige as a wealthy slaveholder to win the necessary approval of the white planters. "You perceive at once," he wrote Mary Jones, "that it [his plan] will be somewhat unpopular, and may excite against me much opposition, and that I shall need great judgment and prudence. . . . You will therefore," he demanded, "take care of this letter, and keep to yourself this plan of mine."[1]

His plan was simple enough: he would form among Liberty County planters a voluntary association for the religious instruction of slaves. It was a plan that had proved itself in other reforms (there was a voluntary society for almost every ill in the nation), but it was a plan that had to be sold to the planters. They might be of Puritan stock, but they lived, after all, in Georgia, not Massachusetts. They had their Temperance Society, but there were no Lyman Beechers among them, much less a Theodore Parker or Horace Mann or Dorothea Dix. No, they were well educated and widely traveled southern planters with broad interests and concerns, but they were still southern planters, first and foremost southern planters. What more prudent and cautious approach, then, than to get friends and family together and make a proposal? This was precisely what Jones did.

They gathered in the little courthouse in the village of Riceboro. Dr. Quarterman, pastor at Midway (no one could accuse him of anything radical or rash!), helped Jones issue the invitations. Twenty-nine planters came, and they represented not only the wealth and leadership of the community, but also some of the most distinguished southern families. There was James Steven Bullock, planter and president of the United States Bank in Savannah. His grandfather had been the first president of the Provincial Congress of Georgia, and there were rumors that he would soon be marrying Senator Elliott's widow. There was Odingsell Hart, probably the richest man in the county, and owner of the beautiful Retreat, the great sea-island plantation near Sunbury. John Dunwoody was here. He had graduated from Yale to return home and run his plantation and marry Bullock's sister Jane. There was Barrington King, a handsome, energetic, and industrious young man who was related to most of the prominent families in the county (he was already talking to them about the opportunities to invest the wealth from his rice plantations in the new Indian lands available in North Georgia). Jones' uncle William Maxwell was also here, having ridden up from his Laurel Hill plantation. A "most elegant gentleman of the olden times," Maxwell had watched Jones as a child spend many happy summer days at the Maxwell cottage on Colonel's Island. All in all, it was a distinguished group of wealthy, pious, and good citizens. But it was also unquestionably a cautious group of white planters.

Jones looked them over with all the earnestness of a young preacher. He had now put behind him the anti-slavery sentiments that had so recently torn at his heart. He had to be cautious in order for his zeal to find a receptive audience: he was, after all, standing before these planters in Riceboro and not writing his fiancée from the North. If only he could do justice to his great theme, if only he could reach the hearts of these friends and neighbors, what an impact it would have! What an opportunity it would be for the religious instruction of black slaves![2]

II

Evangelism was his theme, and his text was "Go ye into all the world and preach the Gospel to every creature." "All the world," Jones reminded his listeners, included not only foreign shores and distant climes, but Liberty County, and "every creature" meant not only white planters but black slaves. Evangelism, said Jones, was a task that was laid upon every Christian, it was a responsibility that could not be avoided. Because black slaves, like their white owners, were creatures of God "moving onward to the retributions of eternity," they needed the gospel presented to them with saving power. They needed their hearts changed and their morals reformed. Could there be any doubt about this when one looked at the condition of many of the slaves in Liberty County?

> They lie, steal, blaspheme; are slothful, envious, malicious, inventors of evil things, deceivers, covenant breakers, implacable, unmerciful. They are greatly wanting in natural affection, improvident, without understanding and grossly immoral. Chastity is an exceedingly rare virtue. Polygamy is common, and there is little

sacredness attached to the marriage contract. It is entered into for the most part without established forms, and is dissolved at the will of the parties: nor is there any sacredness attached to the Sabbath. It is a day of idleness and sleep, of sinful amusements, of visiting, or of labor. They are generally temperate through necessity; when ardent spirits can be obtained, they will freely drink it. Numbers of them do not go to church, and cannot tell us who Jesus Christ is, nor have they ever heard so much as the Ten Commandments read and explained. Of the professors of religion among them, there are many of questionable piety who occasion the different churches great trouble in discipline, for they are extremely ignorant, and frequently are guilty of the grossest vices.[3]

Even the sympathetic white planters must have thought Jones an arrogant young seminarian with much to learn about the human condition. If, however, he felt he had to be prudent about the slavery question, he knew he could be zealous for moral rectitude, he could talk about chastity and sabbath observance and temperance and biblical knowledge. He in later years would mellow as he visited among the sick and dying and grieving, but for now this zealous spirit, this highhanded arrogance, suited his purposes well. For it allowed him to focus upon the morality of the blacks, it gave him an opportunity to call attention to all the behavior of blacks that offended white sensibilities, that called for remedial action. It was an approach that would appeal to white planters, for it meant a major concern would be to socialize the slaves of Liberty County into a southern society of morals and manners.

But if Jones knew how to count the sins of the slaves, he also could accuse the planters as well—with, to be sure, a cautious, prudent accusation. There would be no charge that they were "men-stealers," or that they were involved in an "inhuman abuse of power," but he could say that they had not been responsible as masters. If their black slaves were ignorant and destitute, if they were "a nation of heathen in our very midst," the planters needed to recognize that they had done very little on behalf of the slaves' religious welfare. It would not do for them to dismiss the problem by saying that blacks were somehow incapable of receiving religious instruction. That clearly was not the case, for God had "made of one blood all the nations of men that dwell on the face of the earth." It could not be plainer that "all men have one common origin, and that all are capable of exercising proper affection toward God. . . ." (This was an issue that was only beginning to raise its ugly head. Thomas Smyth, a classmate of Jones at Princeton and the new pastor at the Second Presbyterian Church in Charleston, would in the years ahead be battling those who sought to deny the humanity of the black on the grounds of a dual origin of the races). To verify this common origin, Jones told the planters that they needed only take notice of the blacks around them who understood the gospel and lived lives of exemplary Christian piety.[4]

That was the problem as Jones now perceived it. It was no longer a question of slavery but of the religion and morality of black men and women and the responsibilities of white owners. To deal with this problem, he proposed that a new work be begun for the slaves of Liberty County.

Jones was sure it was a good plan. He had worried over it such a long time and had sought the advice of everyone he could find who would lend an ear: he had talked to Ebenezer Porter and Leonard Woods in Andover and with Samuel Miller, Charles Hodge, and Archibald Alexander in Princeton. He had even made an extended trip to Philadelphia, Washington, and Baltimore to help formulate his plans. He had met with Senator Theodore Frelinghuysen who was immersed in benevolent societies, and spent long hours with R. R. Gurley who was the very personification of the colonization movement. There had even been a special trip to see Benjamin Lundy, the anti-slavery leader and editor of the *Genius of Universal Emancipation.* They had all given him advice; they had all talked about the evils of slavery and the need for action. And Jones had listened to it all, sifted it through his mind and heart where pictures of Liberty County and memories of home were lodged, and out of the residue formulated the plan which he now presented to the planters at Riceboro.[5]

His proposal was that the planters form themselves into a voluntary association and "take the religious instruction of the colored population into their own hands." They would appoint teachers from among their number who would go to stations located near several plantations where the slaves could come for instruction and worship. There during the week and on the Sabbath the teachers would "communicate instruction *orally,* and in as systematic and intelligible a manner as possible, embracing all the principles of the Christian religion as understood by orthodox Protestants, and carefully avoiding all points of doctrine that separate different religious denominations." The teachers would not be sent to any plantation without the "cordial consent of the owner," nor would they appear except at those times specified by him. The wishes and arrangements of the owners were to be "consulted and complied with." Teachers were to "confine themselves to the *religious instruction* of the Negroes wholly." They were not to "intermeddle with the concerns of the plantation in any manner, nor repeat abroad what their ears hear, or their eyes see on them." In addition to the work of the teachers, Jones proposed, not unexpectantly, that "a missionary may be employed to take a general supervision of the whole, occupy Sabbath stations, preach also during the week on plantations, and assist in framing courses of instruction." The planters gathered at Riceboro had, of course, little doubt about the person Jones had in mind to be the missionary to "these heathen" in their midst.[6]

What a prudent plan it was! How carefully it was tailored to calm the fears of white masters: the teachers would be local slaveholders, members of the Association, who had self interest as well as community pressure to safeguard their activities; the instructions would be oral, free from the dangers of teaching slaves to read or write—which was, in any case, illegal; the content would be orthodox Protestantism, exempt from denominational squabbling and safe from the radicalism that often infected the unorthodox; and the activities and conditions of the plantations would be off-limits, beyond the interests or concerns of the visiting teacher or missionary.

But Jones did not stop with these words of assurance. He had to expose himself even more; he had to press on and show his friends that his plan was not only safe but beneficial. There would be a better understanding among both masters and slaves of the mutual relationships that existed between them. In particular, there would be "greater subordination and a decrease of crime amongst the Negroes." There was no need for whites to fear that religious instruction would promote revolts or the desire for freedom and equality. Just the opposite was the case. The teachers themselves would supplement the patrol system which, at any rate, was "not efficiently executed now." (There were few Liberty County whites that wanted to ride about keeping an eye on the blacks!) The simple presence of a white man, however, at "stated times amongst the Negroes," would "tend greatly to the promotion of good order." The plan, said Jones, seemed "to carry our security in it." But more than this external show of authority, there would be an internal change in the heart of the slaves. They would accept the authority of their masters: they would think like slaves, act like slaves, and be slaves. "We believe" said Jones, that the authority of masters "can be strengthened and supported in this way only; for the duty of obedience will never be felt or performed to the extent that we desire it, unless we can *bottom it on religious principle."* That was the key. That was where Jones would encounter the blacks of Liberty County in a theological struggle. For if the blacks would come to believe that obedience to white owners was a religious duty, that submission to their masters was an obligation owed to God, then the authority of the planters would be built upon a solid rock. If, however, blacks resisted that religious principle or substituted another for it, then the authority of masters would be established upon the shifting sands of power and fear.[7]

Jones now took a final, dangerous plunge—he assured his friends and neighbors that, in addition to encouraging good order and subordination among their slaves, religious instruction of blacks would provide economic advantages for slaveholders. A faithful servant, he said, "is more profitable than an unfaithful one. He will do more and better work, be less troublesome, and less liable to disease." Of all the things he said, of all the words he wrote, nothing would come back to haunt him more than this. His work would never be free from the suspicion that at its heart it was guided by economic motivations, that it was an attempt to increase the profits of the planters. Jones knew only too well that he was in dangerous waters and quickly moved to point out that the salvation of the slaves was the primary goal of religious instruction. While economic self-interest might be a powerful motivation in the hearts of white planters, the purpose was the salvation of the slaves' souls. "The great object," Jones declared, "for which we would communicate religious instruction to them is that their souls may be saved. To this all other objects should be subordinated." Jones believed that. It was fundamental for him. It colored all his perceptions about who he was and what he was about. It both gave him courage and patience in trying times and covered his life and his work with grand illusions.[8]

In concluding his address to the white planters of Liberty County, Jones spoke of their responsibility to their slaves. In the providence of God, the blacks had been placed under their care. For this reason they had the heavy responsibility of providing them with religious instruction. Perhaps answering the doubts of his own heart so recently changed from anti-slavery sentiment, Jones declared that slavery itself could be justified if one soul were saved. Speaking as a slaveholder and illustrating the great distance that separated him from the black men and women of Liberty County, he assured his white listeners that it is "certain that the salvation of one soul will more than outweigh all the pain and woe of their capture and transportation, and subsequent residence among us." With such a perspective as this, Jones justified his return to Liberty County and his missionary work among the Georgia slaves.[9]

II

Jones had made his point. He had covered the ground carefully, step by step, so that in the end his friends were convinced and the "Liberty County Association for the Religious Instruction of the Negroes" was formed. They organized that very day. (Jones had all the details carefully arranged so that they had little to do but agree.) No one was surprised when Jones was called to be the missionary for the Association. He had, after all, conceived and organized it to give support to the missionary work he had set his mind and heart on back in Princeton. During his first seven years, he would receive no compensation for his labors. His personal wealth, drawn from the toil of black slaves, would give him the necessary economic freedom for this Liberty County experiment and would allow the Association the necessary time to gain the support of the community.[10]

The Association was the first of its kind in the South, and, as might be expected, it met with initial difficulties. Few people seemed to believe that it would last or that it would be able to accomplish its goals. There was a "general indifference," and while influential planters joined, there were only twenty nine who signed the constitution. Additionally, there was opposition that showered nothing but ridicule or contempt upon the whole project. The greatest difficulty, however, was Jones' own inexperience and the teachers' lack of training. Faced with these difficulties, Jones accepted a call, after only one month of missionary labors, to be the pastor of the First Presbyterian Church in Savannah. He did this, he later recalled, "with the understanding that, whenever I felt prepared, I might withdraw from the church and return to my chosen field." For eighteen months he labored in Savannah with the question of religious instruction of slaves always on his mind. He brought the subject before his white congregation in his sermons, he secured endorsement for the work from the courts of the Presbyterian Church in Georgia and South Carolina, and he constantly referred to the subject in

letters to family and friends. Then, in November, 1832, he returned to his plantation home and began for the second time his
missionary labors among the black slaves of Liberty County.[11]

III

The district of the county in which Jones focused his evangeliza-
tion was approximately 25 miles long and 15 miles wide and
contained between 100 to 125 plantations with 4,577 slaves. In
an effort to reach the slaves scattered among so many plantations,
he divided the district into areas and selected appropriate places
within each area for a "station." Here on alternating Sundays the
blacks would gather for worship.[12]

Jones hoped that the use of stations would solve an important
problem of slave evangelism: how to combine safety with effec-
tiveness? Black preachers and separate churches for slaves were
regarded as a threat to the order and stability of southern society,
for they would involve the loss of white control and discipline
over the slaves and the possible use of religious assemblies for
the plotting of slave revolts. At the same time, however, it was
clear that slaves were destitute of a pastoral ministry. White ministers, for the most part, refused to consider them a part of their
pastoral charge. "They are called to preach to masters," noted
Jones, "and to masters do they preach."[13]

The most effective way, Jones argued, to provide a distinctive
and safe ministry for blacks was through the use of stations.
Blacks and whites would still be joined together in one church
"under the same pastor, having access to the same ordinances,
baptism, and the Lord's Supper, at the same time and place," and
would be subject to "the same care and discipline; the two classes
forming *one* pastoral charge, *one* church, *one* congregation." At
the same time, however, blacks would be allowed to gather at the
stations on select Sundays under the watchful eye of a white
missionary. Here they could sing hymns and hear preaching

adapted to their "circumstances and conditions" rather than sermons prepared for white masters. Here they could claim, in however limited a fashion, a time and place for their own worship.[14]

Jones located the stations in accessible areas where the slave
population was dense. In 1833 six stations were designated by
the Association: Sunbury, Pleasant Grove, Newport, Midway,
Fraser's Plantation, and Walthourville. The last two would never
be successful stations: Fraser's Plantation was too closely associated with plantation work and not enough with church—it
was, in fact, the only station not located next to a church—and
Walthourville was too much of a retreat for the whites. It was here
during the malarial season that the planters came to enjoy the tall
pines and sand hills, and the blacks, knowing that, could never
bring themselves to make it an important location for their worship though some attended a Sunday School here for a number
of years.[15]

Sunbury, overlooking the waters and marshes of the Medway
River, had been for a long time an important place in the religious life of the slaves of Liberty County. At one time the village
itself had been a thriving town with dreams of rivaling Savannah
as the port for Georgia. The church at Midway had a chapel here,
and the Rev. Dr. William McWhir, a doughty Presbyterian from
Ireland, had established on the bank of the Medway the best
school in the state. It was at the Sunbury Baptist Church, however, that the blacks had found a welcomed place. This church
had a long history of interest in the religious instruction of slaves
and many a black had been baptized in the waters of the Medway.
As a boy Jones had seen them, singing and praying, march
in a long line from the little church until they reached the river
bank. The marsh grass stretched out in the distance like green
fields of grain and the great oaks overhead lent their solem-
nity to the occasion. Those who sought baptism confessed
their sins, said they wanted to be saved, and went down into the
waters while the songs of the people blended with the soft sounds
of the current and sea breezes. Charles Scriven, the white minister, plunged them down into the dark water baptising them as the

tide flowed out carrying their sins away.[16]

The church building at Sunbury, constructed in 1810, included a gallery for the slaves where in 1816 a Sunday School had been started with the purpose of teaching the slaves how to read the Scriptures (it had lasted only a few months since the Georgia legislature passed a law that same year forbidding such instructions). During the early years of the Liberty County Association, the Rev. Samuel S. Law, Baptist minister at Sunbury and vice-president of the Association, supplied this station and labored among the blacks of the area. Later, when the Baptists were without a minister, Jones would make the old village one of his regular stations.[17]

Further inland, west of Riceboro in the piney woods above the North Newport River, was another Baptist church. It too was conveniently situated for the baptism of believers. Here the waters were much sweeter than by the marshes of Medway, and the surrounding plantations grew no rice but a fine cotton cared for by a large slave population. Beside the Newport Baptist Church, Jones established one of his most successful stations. The blacks loved this place and would make it in the years following emancipation a center of their community. But for now, they came to the station to hear a white preacher to black slaves.[18]

Between the two branches of the Newport, about five miles south of Riceboro, there was a small meeting house that was selected for a station. Surrounded by great live oaks it carried, as did a hundred such places throughout the South, the name Pleasant Grove. The building had been used for a while by Methodist circuit riders who preached here to both blacks and whites, but in 1833 it had become a station for the plantation slaves of the vicinity. Crowding into the small building, they had flowed out of the doors and around the corners to stand by open windows and hear Jones preach and teach. In 1840 Jones requested a new building. With the endorsement of the Association, a subscription had been taken and in a short time a new church building had been dedicated before a congregation of 50 whites and 300 blacks. Within the next three years the number attending had doubled, although the membership of the church remained small.[19]

The final station, and the most important one, was at the Midway Congregational Church. Here Jones built upon the work of both white and black predecessors. Robert Quarterman, following the practice of earlier pastors at Midway, had held Sunday afternoon services for blacks, while several of the white officers had conducted Sunday afternoon services at a nearby plantation. Black preachers, however, were the real predecessors to Jones' work at Midway. Towards the end of the 18th century, Mingo, a freed man living on Mr. Peter Winn's plantation, had begun preaching to the blacks of the area with the approval of the church. They would meet in the piney woods a short way from the Midway Church. "The place was fitted up with booths of bushes with wide seats and a raised platform in the center, on which Mingo stood, called 'the stand.'" Mingo would preach between the morning and afternoon services held at the Midway Church. He also "held meetings at some of the plantations, and notably among them, on that of Mr. John Lambert, who felt a lively interest in the race, and engaged him to hold meetings regularly and statedly during his life time, on account of which, his plantation became a place of meeting for the negroes of the neighborhood. . . ."

The Lambert plantation was an unusual place with a history intimately associated with the Midway station. John Lambert had been one of the first Liberty County planters after the Revolutionary War to allow the religious instruction of his slaves. At his death in 1785 his will had stated that the income from his plantation and slaves was to be used for charitable purposes designated by the Midway Church. For the next fifty-three years, the labors of Scipio and John, of Prince, Ned, and other Lambert slaves would provide for the widows and orphans and struggling students of the white community. At the same time, however, the plantation itself would become a center of the black community. When Mingo died, Jack, a slave in the Lambert estate, was bought by the Midway Church so that he could preach and "give himself wholly to the work." He was followed by Sharper, who was owned by Mrs. Quarterman, the wife of the minister at Midway. Sharper preached at the Midway "stand" as his predecessors had done and "labored more abundantly than they all, holding meetings at the plantations of Mr. Lambert, Mr. James and others." He was a black leader who was trusted not only by the slaves, but the planters as well. Little is known of him other than the time he served as a black preacher and the high regard in which he was held. He did, no doubt, help the blacks love and value each other as they responded in love to him. And, no doubt, he taught of God's love for all his children. In as much as he did this, he helped the black slaves of Liberty County both set limits to the degradations of slavery and shape a faith to sustain them in a weary land. He died in 1833 "full of years and universally lamented." His funeral was held at night on the green in front of the Midway Church. A large number of slaves gathered. "At the close of the service," wrote Jones, "we opened the coffin. The moon shone on his face. The people gazed upon it and lifted up their voices and wept. His sons bore him to his grave. In silence we returned to our homes oppressed with grief at this heavy affliction of God."[20]

The work of acknowledged and public black preachers would be severely limited in Liberty County after the death of Sharper. Their labors were regarded by concerned whites as somewhat spasmodic—as was the work of white ministers among black slaves lacking "a regular systematic training and instruction." More to the point, however, was the growing defensiveness of southern whites and the increasing fears brought on by the slave revolt of the black preacher Nat Turner.[21]

In 1833 Jones, the white missionary, moved into the pulpit once occupied by Mingo, Jack, and Sharper, and thereby removed one of the few fragile areas of black independence in Liberty County. The following year the Georgia legislature would outlaw black preachers. In 1838 the Lambert plantation would be sold and the proceeds invested in securities. There would be trouble on the plantation after the death of Sharper.

Runaways would begin to be reported—a relatively rare occurrence in Liberty County—and the management of the estate would become more difficult and troublesome. So the plantation and its slaves would be sold to a local planter. Three years later, the trustee would begin to use a portion of the income to provide support for Jones' missionary labors. In the years to come the Lambert Estate, secured through the sale of slaves and plantation, would become a major financial support for the Liberty County Association for the Religious Instruction of Negroes, and funds from it would be provided so that the old open bush arbor at the Midway station where the black preachers had labored could be replaced by an enclosed shed with floors and benches. Further renovation, it was said, made it "very comfortable" both to white preachers and black slaves.[22]

3

More Than Guards, Guns, and Bayonets

I

Early on a spring morning in 1841, when the sky was still silver with predawn mist and the lawn of Montevideo was damp with dew, the orchards and groves surrounding the plantation erupted with the songs of woodland birds welcoming the new day. The mockingbird, weary from a night of singing, gave a glorious conclusion to its haunting southern melody. The woodpecker beat its steady drum, knocking bark to the ground, while the thrush filled the air with an aria of joy, and doves cooed their sad songs. A cool breeze gathered over the waters of the North Newport and carried the fragrance of the low country up toward Montevideo. Then the golden dawn, rising with smoke from the plantation kitchen, revealed a sabbath morning for Charles Colcock Jones, missionary to black slaves of Liberty County.

Jones was already up and dressed. His private devotions were followed by breakfast served by the slave Marcia who, no doubt, had prepared most of the day's food the night before to avoid breaking the sabbath rest. Gilbert, who was in charge of the stables, brought Jones' horse around to the front door. Gathering his Bible, catechism, and sermon material, Jones mounted the horse and rode the sandy roads of Liberty County to Midway, the station appointed for that day.

The first service of the Sabbath was the early morning prayer meeting.[1] Jones entered the Midway shed and went up to the "stand." Already a number of blacks had gathered from the nearby plantations. Lengthening spring days gave the extra sunlight needed for this early service that focused upon slave participation. A hymn was sung. Jones then called upon some prominent black to lead in prayer. He knew that whomever he called upon would not ask to be excused, but would rise up and give "utterance to the thoughts and desires of his heart as he was able." They were often deeply moving prayers, especially those of Dembo, a native of Africa, and a member of the Midway Church. When this black man closed his prayers, Jones frequently felt as "weak as water" and thought "that I ought not to open my mouth in public, and indeed, knew not what it was to pray." Such prayers as these along with a Scripture reading, a few practical remarks by Jones, and another hymn would mark the beginning of the sabbath day services.[2]

After the prayer meeting, the blacks would rest and visit and watch the whites arriving in carriages and on horseback for the service in the Midway Church. There was Dr. Quarterman, tall and grey-headed, dressed in his old fashioned double-breasted cutaways, and still carrying with dignity the good looks of his youth. He had grown up in the church and had now served it as pastor for the last eighteen years. With him was the Reverend I.S.K. Axson, co-pastor, an Icabod of a man, completely bald on top with thick curls on the sides covering his ears and accentuating the sharp, angular features of his face. He arrived with his family having traveled the twelve miles from Jonesville in a carriage. Then there were the LeContes and the McIntoshes, the Mallards, the Varnedoes and Maxwells, the Ways and Osgoods and all the Baker clan. As these and other whites arrived from their plantations and entered the church, their black slaves returned to the shed for the main service of the day.[3]

Jones had a carefully prepared sermon for his black congregation. He was convinced that his preaching had to be especially adapted to the blacks who had been culturally deprived, neglected by white ministers, and left unlettered because of the laws of the state. Yet he thought that with "proper pains" he could "speedily carry them, ignorant as they are conceived to be, to the limits of our actual knowledge of the doctrines of Christianity: and what is more, make them know and feel it."[4] Such preaching, Jones believed, was a difficult task requiring highly qualified men. It was a serious mistake to think that any ignorant white could preach to blacks. Success demanded "well educated and as intelligent ministers and good preachers" as the church could supply.[5] In the same way, if a minister was of the opinion that "any sort of sermon" would do for black congregations, "let him try it" Jones had warned, "and he will presently be of another mind." He knew his black congregations were "good judges of a good sermon," as well as "proud enough" not to accept poor sermons. It was necessary, Jones was convinced, for the preacher to slaves to "study just as profoundly, and as extensively, as he who preaches to whites."[6]

Jones' first step in preparing such sermons was to study the "habits of thoughts, superstitions and manners" of the slaves so that he could bridge as best he could the gulf that separated white preachers and black slaves. Yet he was fully aware that whites did not know blacks at a significant depth, and that it was extremely difficult to acquire such intimate knowledge given the blinding prejudices that shaped white perception. For this reason he spent long hours studying the history, traditions, and folkways of his black parishioners.[7] There were studies on West Africa to be read —Beacham's book on the Gold Coast and the Ashanti, Lieutenant Forbe's work on the Dehomi, Freeman's *Journal* and Duncan's *Travels*. But above all there were the reports of John Leighton Wilson, friend and great missionary at Cape Palmas and the Gaboon. They were not simply the pious stories of a missionary, but careful studies of African history and culture that would win

Wilson a place in the Royal Oriental Society of Great Britain and
be gathered together into the encyclopedia *Western Africa: Its History, Condition, and Prospects.* (Livingston would say that it was the
best book ever written on that part of Africa.) It was, however,
not African history but Afro-American history that demanded
most of Jones' attention. He gathered everything he could find:
reports and pamphlets, rare books and obscure records. He
would use them all to write his own *The Religious Instruction of the
Negroes in the United States* that would remain for over a hundred
years the best source on the subject. All of it was used to help him
understand his black parishioners, to try to bridge the gap between preacher and listener.[8]

Jones believed, however, for a sermon to be good, it must be
biblical, and so he turned to a critical examination of the Hebrew
and Greek texts. There was a wide variety of commentaries; he
would recommend for those attempting to preach to slaves
Henry's *Commentary,* Andrew Fuller's *Lectures on Genesis,* Porteus'
Lectures on Matthew, Scott's *Commentary,* Stuard on Hebrews, and
Hodge on Romans. He was serious about his sermon preparation
and spent hours preparing them. But he never raised questions
about his hermeneutics. He never seemed to wonder how his
white eyes might influence what he found in his study.[9]

Jones wrote his sermons in full manuscript form. There would
be no outline to be given flesh and blood while he was preaching
—much less a noteless or extemporaneous sermon! No, he wrote
it all out with a handsome hand and on narrow paper, but with
a clear threefold division: an introduction of three to six pages,
an exposition of the text that often ran to more than fifty pages,
and a conclusion of five to ten pages on what had been learned.
Sermons intended for black slaves should be, he wrote, "plain in
language, simple in construction, and pointed in application, and
of any length *from a half hour to an hour and a quarter,* according to
the subject and interest of the people."[10]

When Jones began preaching, he sought to make his delivery
"grave, solemn, dignified, free from affection, hauteur, or familiarity, yet ardent and animated." He reflected the Midway congregations' disdain for any kind of revivalism and their suspicion

of emotional excesses. They wanted, after all, sermons suited for their neat meeting house: logical, solid as a heart-of-pine, and with a simple grace. It was, of course, a theological position well suited to maintain control and order with a large assembly of slaves, and Jones expected a "dignified and restrained" response from his black listeners. There were to be no *"audible* expressions of feeling in the way of groanings, cries, or noises of any kind." There were to be no "amens!" to his sermons, no moaning that could spread throughout the congregation with a low hum gathering strength until it broke forth like lightning over the waving marsh. No, the focus was definitely cerebral, the tone subdued, but that was not all to his sermons. There was also a passion, a pious zeal, that reached out to the heart as well as the head. And somehow, strange as it seems, in the preaching and the listening, some at least of the gulf between the white preacher and the black slave was bridged.[11]

The black congregation at the Midway station knew full well by 1841 that they could expect Jones to preach on a variety of subjects. He had always been concerned, because of the illiteracy of his hearers, to present as much of the biblical narrative as possible and had dealt extensively with parables, historical events, and biographies.[12] His favorite theme, however, was the conversion of lost souls from sin to salvation. It was for him the great theme of the Scriptures, the message to the nations, and the focus of most of his sermons. There had been messages on the hope of heaven, on "The Salvation of the Soul," and "Lay Not Up for Yourselves Treasures Upon the Earth," and heart-shaking sermons upon the dangers of hell, sermons that warned that "The Wicked Shall be Turned into Hell, and All the Nations that Forget God," and that reminded not only Liberty County slaves, but white congregations before whom he preached in both the South and North that "When a Wicked Man Dieth, His Expectations Shall Perish." In these Jones did not hesitate to describe the tortured existence of souls burning in eternal lakes of fires. It was, he said, what unbelieving whites and blacks could both expect.[13]

There had been other sermons, however, that had been aimed

more directly at the daily lives of the black congregation gathered at Midway. In particular, there had been a series of sermons on the duties of servants to earthly masters. Built around the stories of biblical slaves, these sermons were intended to "inculcate respect, obedience and fidelity to masters, as duties, for the discharge of which they as servants would have to account to God in the great day." There was Eliezer, Abraham's servant, who was a model slave: he took care of Abraham's property, he would not offend God by becoming a thief, and he was both a faithful and diligent worker. He was all that any good master would want and his reward was great not only in heaven, but also on earth, as he was chosen to be the chief among Abraham's slaves.[14]

In contrast to Eliezer, there was Gehazi, Elisha's servant, who stood as a warning to all disobedient and unfaithful slaves: he was a thief, a liar, and completely untrustworthy. He was all that any good master abhorred. For these sins God had made him a leper, an outcast, a wanderer among the desert places. There was no escaping God, Jones had warned his slave congregation, for even secret sins were seen by the Heavenly Master.[15]

The most famous of all the biblical slaves, however, was Onesimus, the run-away slave of Philemon. Jones, and no doubt his black listeners at Midway, still remembered vividly what had happened when the white preacher had taken Onesimus for his text:

> I was preaching to a large congregation on the Epistle of Philemon and when I insisted upon fidelity and obedience as Christian virtues in servants and upon the authority of Paul, condemned the practice of *running away,* one half of my audience deliberately rose up and walked off with themselves, and those that remained looked anything but satisfied, either with the preacher or his doctrine.

At the close of the service, the remaining slaves had expressed anger and contempt toward Jones and his ideas. Several had agreed "that there was no such an Epistle in the Bible," others had said that such a message "was not the Gospel," while some had insisted that Jones preached only "to please the masters," and had declared that they would not come to hear him preach again. It was for the black slaves a dangerous and amazing display of open resistance to a powerful white slaveholder. But more than this, it was a challenge to the theological presuppositions and paternalistic assumptions of the white preacher. It was a challenge to the authority of his understanding of the Scriptures, and even more, the authority of the Apostle Paul, for, they said, such a message "was not the Gospel." That was what made it such an amazing and dangerous challenge, for it meant these black slaves had a theological perspective to stand over against that of the whites, one which could provide them with an alternative to the "religious principle" Jones had said was necessary in order for the slaves to accept not simply the power but also the authority of masters. Jones apparently never asked himself the origin of this resistance. If he had, he no doubt would have discovered that his predecessors, black and white, had helped to provide a theological foundation by which the slaves of Liberty County could judge what was the gospel and what was not. And part of the irony of Jones' own work would be that he would help to strengthen that foundation while at the same time he sought to instill a sense of duty and submission in the hearts of the slaves.[16]

Jones had not attempted to answer the criticism, but had gone about his work "as though nothing had happened." In a short while most of the displeased slaves were back at the station listening once again to him. Two years later he had reassured the Association that "with an increase of knowledge they will hear such preaching now." Still, some slaves had continued to object to Jones as a preacher because he was a slaveholder and "his people have to work as well as we," and Jones would later warn others that it was inexpedient and unfair to dwell on the duties of slaves. It had been an important lesson for him, revealing in an usually clear manner both something of the hidden life and perspectives of the black slaves and something about how far he could go as a white preacher. Duties could be mentioned, but not too often. Christian ethics generally applied, he would later say, would meet most of the needs of the plantation without "harping" on the duties.[17]

One of the important thrusts of Jones' preaching was against the remnants of African religious beliefs among the isolated black people of Liberty County. Whatever part these played in providing strength for resisting the oppression and degradation of slavery is not clear, but they were an important aspect of slave belief. Voodoo was still a powerful force filling the world of the slaves with numerous supernatural powers. Root doctors and sorcerers, wizards and witches were looked upon with respect and fear. There were the witches who changed their shape at night, slipped into houses and rode on people's chests so that the victims awoke feeling not only terrified but as if they were smothering. There were the charms of black cat ashes and bones, graveyard dirt and hair, nail clippings and blood root. There were "plat-eye" ghosts and headless spirits, conjure bags to be worn around the neck for protection, and frizzled chickens to be left in the yard to dig up dangerous charms; and there were the stories of slaves who suddenly sprang into the air and flew back to Africa, and tales of hoes that worked by themselves. It was all part of a secret world for the slaves, usually beyond the sight of the whites, but always lurking in the shadows of slave culture to emerge only in the folkways and the art of the people.[18]

In an early sermon entitled "Simon the Sorcerer," Jones had attacked the reality of such supernatural forces and dismissed the power of sorcerers, wizards, and witches. Yet Jones had not hesitated to teach about Satan's power and to paint grim pictures of hell. He would soon be preaching a sermon entitled "The Person and Character: Occupation and Influence of the Wicked One: And the Duty of Christians in Respect Therto." Satan was at work in this world, Jones would declare, tempting the lonely slave to sin and disobedience in the daily life on the plantation. Such sermons were both moves against superstitions and fear, and calls for the acknowledgment of sin and guilt. As such, and inasmuch as they were directed to slaves, they were attempts to facilitate the adjustment of blacks to their place in a slave society.[19]

The sermon which Jones now preached in the spring of 1841 to the black congregation at Midway was entitled "Our Lord

Cleans The Temple." Unlike some of the earlier, more contro-
versial, sermons, this one had the simple theme of the proper way
to behave in church. Giving a long list of what not to do, Jones
stressed the point that the church service was not a place for
social life. The sermon's very simplicity, however, reflected
Jones' continuing efforts to transform the behavior of the black
slave to meet the needs and expectations of white planters. As his
black congregation listened to him explain the mannerly way to
behave in church, they were learning something of what it meant
to be obedient, virtuous, and profitable slaves—at least that was
part of what Jones hoped and expected.[20]

II

When the preaching service was over, the black congregation
went out under the surrounding oaks and pines for a mid-day
meal. For some it may have been simply a sweet potato cooked
before an open fire. For the more fortunate, there may have been
fish caught in a tidal creek, or rabbit trapped in a gum, or perhaps
even chicken or pork or rice. The white families, worshipping
across the road at Midway, came out of the church and went to
the little houses, or booths, which they had erected for places of
rest and refreshment during the intermission between morning
and afternoon services. Baskets were brought out with "abundant 'cold snacks,' " and quick naps were taken before the second
sermon of the day.[21]

In the early afternoon Jones began the Sabbath school classes.
This work was perhaps the most important of all his missionary
labors. He had understood from the first that he must evangelize
the slave children if he were to convert many of the blacks to
Christianity and help them adjust to their role as obedient "servants" in southern society. The schools were, he believed, the
"great hope" for the religious instruction of slaves, and he had
been vigorous in their promotion not only in Liberty County but

throughout the South. To the planters, he had said, "These *children* are to be your future *men*-servants and *women*-servants, they will serve you more faithfully for early religious instruction." But the slaves themselves had also recognized that the schools were an opportunity and that they could perhaps be used for their own purposes as they taught them, in a limited way, of a broader world and a God who brought judgment upon masters as well as slaves. The opening of the Sabbath schools, Jones reported, had "electrified the people: it put a new face upon their religious state: it formed a new era in their advance of knowledge and virtue." Such a response reflected their awareness that whatever purposes the whites might have in the establishment of such schools, that education, even of a limited kind, was a source of power and resistance for the blacks.[22]

There were approximately one hundred and fifty blacks who gathered at the Midway shed for the afternoon Sabbath school class. The hour began with singing. Jones had found that the black slaves were "extravagantly fond of music" and he had made the teaching of hymns an important part of the afternoon's lesson.[23] The hymns, however, were carefully selected, for Jones hoped they would not only help teach the Christian tradition, but also destroy or at least push underground the blacks' African heritage and indigenous music.

There were, for example, the shout songs, more incantation than song, mystic, powerful, and clearly of African origin. A number of dancers would form a circle and move counterclockwise to a rhythmic step: feet flat on the floor, heels tapping, hips swaying, shoulders stiff, arms close to the body, hands forward with palms up as a supplication and all the while an undulating flow of song:

> Day, day Oh—see day's a-comin'
> > Ha'k 'e angels
> Day, day Oh—see day's a-comin'
> > Ha'k 'e angels
> Oh look at day (ha'k 'e angels)—Oh Lord
> > Ha'k 'e angels

Look out de windah (ha'k 'e angels)—Oh Lord
    Ha'k 'e angels
Look out de windah (ha'k 'e angels)—Oh Lord
    Ha'k 'e angels
See day's a-comin (ha'k 'e angels)—Oh Lord
    Ha'k 'e angels
Look out de windah (ha'k 'e angels)—Oh Lord
    Ha'k 'e angels
Look out de windah (ha'k 'e angels)—Oh Lord
    Ha'k 'e angels
Call my mother (ha'k 'e angels)—Oh Lord
    Ha'k 'e angels
Throw off de covah (ha'k 'e angels)—Oh Lord
    Ha'k 'e angels
Start that a-risin' (ha'k 'e angels)—Oh Lord
    Ha'k 'e angels
Who that a-comin' (ha'k 'e angels)—Oh Lord
    Ha'k 'e angels
Look out de windah (ha'k 'e angels)—Oh Lord.

Sometimes there was even more dramatic participation in the song. In "Down to the Mire," dancers took turns in the center of the ring on their knees, heads touching the floor, rotating with the circle while the passing shouters pushed the head "down to the mire."

Sister Emma, Oh, you mus' come down to de mire.
Sister Emma, Oh, you mus' come down to de mire.
    Jesus been down
        to de mire
    You must bow low
        to de mire
    Honor Jesus
        to de mire
    Honor Jesus
        to de mire
    Lowrah lowrah
        to de mire
    Lowrah lowrah
        to de mire
    Lowrah lowrah
        to de mire

> Jesus been down
> to de mire.[25]

And there were others, many others—work songs and field holl-ers, songs to dance the "Buzzard Lope" and songs to sing for ring games. And there were the spirituals, deeply moving cries of the heart that spoke of faith and courage in a weary land:

> My God is a rock in a weary land
> weary land
> in a weary land
> My God is a rock in a weary land
> Shelter in a time of storm.[26]

Jones liked none of them; he was suspicious of all of them. They were too African, dangerously extravagant, too much, he thought, of the heart and passion, and not enough of the head and reason. And perhaps, just perhaps, he heard hidden within these songs both resistance to subordination and profound spiritual insights that cut through his pretensions, that his own heart could not face.

What would he hear in these poignant lines?

> I know moon-rise, I know star-rise,
>   Lay dis body down.
> I walk in de moonlight, I walk in de starlight,
>   To lay dis body down.
> I'll walk in de graveyard, I'll walk through de graveyard,
>   To lay dis body down.
> I'll lie in de grave and stretch out my arms;
>   Lay dis body down.
> I go to de judgment in de evenin' of de day,
>   When I lay dis body down;
> And my soul and your soul will meet in de day
>   When I lay dis body down.[27]

Who would he think was wrestling in "Wrestlin' Jacob"?

> O wrestlin' Jacob, Jacob, day's a-breakin';
>   I will not let thee go!
> O wrestlin' Jacob, Jacob, day's a-breakin';
>   He will not let me go!
> O, I hold my brudder wid a tremblin' hand;
>   I would not let him go!

> I hold my sister wid a tremblin' hand;
>   I would not let her go!
>
> O, Jacob do hang from a tremblin' limb,
>   He would not let him go!
> O, Jacob do hang from a tremblin' limb,
>   De Lord will bless my soul.
> O wrestlin' Jacob, Jacob, [etc., etc.][28]

Or what sinner could find "no hiding place" before the awful presence of the Lord?

> O Lord, O Lord! what shall we do?
> What shall we do, what shall we do?
> What shall we do for a hiding place;
> No hiding place for sinner here.
> We run to de sea—de sea run dry;
> We run to de rock—de rock do sink;
> We run to de tree—de tree ketch fire;
> We run to de grave—de grave bus open;
> We run to de door—de door shut close;
> We wring we hands, we grine we teet,
> We cry O Lord, O Lord, O Lord
> No hiding place for sinner here.[29]

At any rate, Jones rejected them all and sought to replace them with the hymns of white Protestantism. "One great advantage," he had told planters, "in teaching them good psalms and hymns, is that they are thereby induced to lay aside the extravagant and nonsensical chants, and catches and hallelujah songs of their own composing; and when they sing, which is very often while about their business or of an evening in their houses, they will have something profitable to sing."[30]

The hymns that Jones taught were for the most part hymns of evangelical Protestantism and included such titles as "Jesus, thou heavenly stranger," "There Is a Fountain Filled with Blood," "Blow Ye the Trumpet, Blow," and "Glory to Thee My God This Night." Jones was particularly fond of Watts' hymns which he found the blacks readily learned: "Lord in the Morning Thou Shall Hear," "Behold the Morning Sun," "There Is a God Who Reigns Above," "When I Can Read My Title Clear," "Jesus with

All Thy Saints Above," "I'm Not Ashamed to Own My Lord," and "Now in the Heart of Youthful Blood."[31]

After the opening hymns, Jones read the Scripture lesson. He used "Scripture Cards" with pictures illustrating biblical events to aid in the exposition of the passage. A prayer followed and then the students were asked to repeat from memory the Lord's Prayer, the Apostles' Creed, the Ten Commandments, and selected verses of Scripture. A new hymn was taught—words first and tune second. The last week's lesson was reviewed, followed once more with singing. Then came the time for the catechectical lesson of the day. After the lesson there was a prayer and a final hymn before dismissal.[32]

Jones had found from the first that the black students were eager learners. They were, he had reported to the white owners, "as much interested and as apt at receiving knowledge, as children of any colour under similar circumstances. . . ." After only two years in the Sabbath schools they had been able to recite from memory twenty to thirty pages in the catechism as well as a variety of other lessons.[33]

The ability of the blacks to learn with only oral instruction was an encouragement to Jones. Those whites who "despised" it, he declared, were "without knowledge and without experience of its unspeakable importance and value." Yet Jones was aware of the severe limitations that oral instruction and illiteracy presented in teaching Christian doctrine and duty. He had found it a "peculiar and great difficulty" when the "only access the people have to the light is through the *living* teacher." For Jones, the Protestant minister, there was a serious problem with keeping slaves illiterate, for that meant that they would have only limited access to the Scriptures. In a catechism he prepared for blacks and whites, he declared that those "who would keep the Bible from their fellow creatures, are the enemies of God and man. The Bible belongs of right to every man. It is the property of the world."[34]

Jones, however, was not simply a Protestant minister, he was also a southern planter, a slave owner, working among slaves only through the permission of their white owners. This meant that oral instruction was the only possible method of religious instruction of slaves in Liberty County. Because of this "peculiar and great difficulty," Jones turned to the oral use of catechisms as the best method for teaching black slaves.

III

As the Sabbath school was the central place for Jones' religious instruction of the slaves, the catechism was his most important tool for teaching. By using the catechism orally he both met the requirements of southern law and custom that prohibited slaves from reading and placed himself in control of the material, teaching the blacks what he wanted them to know of the Christian faith and of their duties as slaves.[35]

When Jones had begun his missionary labors in Liberty County, he was unable to find any satisfactory books to aid him in his teaching. He had searched for material on the history of the religious instruction of slaves and had found it scattered and hard to find. He had looked for reports of what others had done: what had succeeded and what had failed, what had won the confidence of planters and what had touched the hearts of slaves—but it was all so fragmentary, so lacking in order and helpful continuity. So he had determined that what he could not find he would do for himself and help to fill the gap for others. For the next thirteen years he would publish his Annual Reports to the Liberty County Association and see that they were printed in leading religious periodicals; he would preach sermons on the subject and deliver addresses and write pamphlets of "Suggestions on the Religious Instruction of the Negroes in the Southern States" and have them all published. He would write his history of *The Religious Instruction of the Negroes In the United States* (it would be his most scholarly work, but filled with passion for his cause), and finally he would fill his greatest need by writing his own catechisms.

There were other catechisms, of course. There were the

Shorter and the Larger Westminster: the former, Jones had learned as a child, the latter he had labored over as a seminarian, and both he had received and adopted in an ordination vow as "containing the system of doctrine taught in the Holy Scriptures." But they were ponderous and scholastic, declaring God to be "a Spirit, infinite, eternal, and unchangeable, in his being, wisdom, power, holiness, justice, goodness, and truth." Such answers were surely solemn enough to insure both the boredom of the pupils and the failure of the Sabbath schools as generations of Presbyterians would rise up and attest. But more than this, they were answers forged in the midst of a political revolution, when Puritans were about the task of violently overthrowing the government of Charles I. They were definitely not the kind of questions and answers one used with slaves.

There were other chatechisms, however, that had been written especially for slaves. William Capers had recently completed one for the Methodist mission to slaves in South Carolina, but it was too short and intended primarily for little children. Benjamin Palmer at the Congregational Church in Charleston had prepared a catechism for the blacks in his congregation and throughout the city, but it would never do for what Jones wanted: there was too much that was omitted, too many areas of Christian faith and life had been ignored. Jones had tried these and others but found none that were "well adapted" to the slaves' condition and circumstances, and so he had written *A Catechism for Colored Persons,* a 108-page manual reflecting his concern for both the salvation of the slaves' souls and their duties to white masters. The supply had soon been exhausted, and, in 1837, Jones revised the catechism and republished it as *A Catechism, of Scripture, Doctrine and Practice, for Families and Sabbath Schools, Designed also for the Oral Instruction of Colored Persons.* Written for both blacks and whites, it soon became widely used throughout the South and was translated—without the sections on slavery—into three other languages for missionary use. It was this catechism which acted as the Bible for the Midway Sabbath School in 1841.[36]

An evangelical presentation of the faith was clearly the primary intent of the whole book. God was presented as the creator and lawgiver who offers salvation to humanity through the death of his son Jesus Christ. Working against God were Satan and his fallen angels. Humanity, fallen through Adam's sin, is saved through belief in Jesus Christ. "It does not matter," Jones taught, "what country one comes from, whether we are from the East or from the West, the North or the South. It does not matter of what *colour* we are, whether of white, or brown, or black. It does not matter of what *condition* we are, whether rich or poor, old or young, male or female, bond or free. Jesus is able to save *all* who come unto him."[37] It was orthodox, evangelical Protestantism. Yet within this evangelical presentation there was a difference, and the difference was slavery.

Jones taught in the Sabbath schools a distinctive doctrine of God. He began with God's omniscience and built a doctrine to undergird strict control of the slaves' behavior:

Q. Is God present in every place?
A. Yes.
Q. What does he see and know?
A. All things.
Q. Who is in duty bound to have justice done Servants when they are wronged or abused or ill-treated by anyone?
A. The Master.
Q. Is it right for the Master to punish his servants cruelly?
A. No.

The questions and answers which then followed presented the masters as those who should not threaten their servants and who should provide them with religious instruction. God is said to be the master of us all in heaven. He does not show favor to earthly masters who will have to "render an account for the manner in which they treat their servants."[41]

The black Sabbath school students, after repeating these benevolent and paternal duties of their owners, then recited their own duties as loyal and faithful "servants":

Q. What command has God given to Servants, concerning obedience to their Masters?

A. "Servants obey in all things your Masters according to the flesh, not in eye-service as men-pleasers, but in singleness of heart, fearing God."

Q. What are Servants to count their Masters worthy of?

A. "All honor."

Q. How are they to do their service of their master?

A. "*With good will,* doing service unto the Lord and not unto men."

Q. How are they to try to please their Masters?

A. "Please them well in all things, not answering again."

Q. Is it right in a Servant when commanded to be sullen and slow, and answer his Master again?

A. "No."

In the questions and answers which followed, the students heard that they were to be an example to other "servants" in their love and obedience to their masters. Masters who were unjust were to be patiently endured. St. Paul and the slave Onesimus were used to forbid running away and the harboring of runaways. Servants were not to lie or steal from their masters. If they did their duty and served God in their station as servants, they would be respected by men and women and blessed and honored by God.[42]

It was an ideal picture of a paternalistic society which the black catechumens memorized—a picture that would make, Jones hoped, for a static harmony and peace at Montevideo and the other plantations of Liberty County. Whites and blacks each had their place in society and each had their responsibilities: whites were owners and masters; blacks were slaves and servants.

IV

When the black slaves had finished their lessons in evangelical piety and had recited to Jones the duties of masters and slaves, they left the Midway station to walk the sandy roads that led back to their plantation quarters. There were a few older men, however, who remained behind for an important meeting. These were the watchmen, the leaders in the black community, "Elders in Israel," respected for their piety and their authority among the blacks. As early as 1811 they had been officially recognized by the Midway Church. Each watchman had responsibility for one or two plantations where he conducted evening prayers for the slaves, kept an eye upon the morals of the black church members, and sought to maintain discipline in the slave community.[43]

These men who gathered with Jones after the Sabbath day service had assumed the positions of leadership that had once been held by the black preachers Mingo, Jack, and Sharper. There was Sam, who was the chief watchman. A slave of Samuel Spencer, Sam had been hired by the session of the Midway Church in 1831, the year Jones was serving the First Presbyterian Church in Savannah, and had been authorized "to act as chief watchman and teacher and preacher over the coloured members of the church." Placed under the supervision of a white elder of the church, Sam was provided with a horse, food, and clothing for the year. In 1838, when Jones was away from his missionary labors teaching at the seminary in Columbia, the slave Toney had been given responsibilities similar to those of Sam in 1831 as well as wages for those days when he had to report to the session on his activities.[44]

Sam and Toney, along with the other watchmen, had originally resisted Jones' efforts among the Liberty County blacks. They had seem him—no doubt correctly—as a threat to their influence and to the fragile independence of their people's religious life. Yet once it had become clear that Jones had the power and authority of the white community behind him and that he was, in many ways, their advocate in the white community, they gave him their support at the stations and on the plantations. This support was a reflection of their realism. They knew both the military power of the whites and the needs of their own people. They therefore sought to work with Jones in ways that would help blacks remember at a deep inner level their worth as persons and their unity as a people held in bondage. Yet their willingness to compromise, however realistic it may have been, was a reflection of their acceptance of slavery. In as much as it was that, it showed the depths of their oppression.[45]

In March of 1840, Jones had begun regular monthly meetings with black watchmen. They gathered in the front of the shed to perform the duties of a church court. If a church member were accused of some offense, the watchmen listened to the testimony of witnesses, examined the accused, and then delivered a verdict. If the case was serious enough for excommunication, they collected and prepared the evidence and presented it before the white session which alone had authority to excommunicate.[46]

There was, for example, the case of Quanimo, who appeared before the watchmen and confessed that he had killed a hog that had not belonged to him. It was such an easy thing to do in the lonely woods of Liberty and such a feast! He was suspended. Then there was Tenah and her problems with Sandy, the slave of Mrs. William Jones, and with Dick, the slave of Mr. Dunwoody. Their difficulties were reported to the session by the watchmen and Dick was told not to communicate with Tenah nor to stay at her house at Mr. McCullough's during the night. A few months later Sandy was suspended because of improper conduct toward her. Tenah herself, after several warnings about her behavior, was excommunicated two years later. And then there was Ishmael who was having difficulties with his wife. After a time of separation, they were reconciled through the efforts of a watchman. It was not unusual for the watchmen to hear cases involving differences among slaves, marital problems, adultery, and stealing. In addition, they were responsible for making recommendations in regard to those blacks who wanted to join the church. In all of this, the watchmen acted as leaders not only in the church but also in the black community as they exercised power and authority in their decision making.[47]

While Jones hoped that the use of the watchmen meetings would save "much unpleasant discipline . . . to the church," and would provide an important means of control among the slaves, these meetings also provided the blacks an important opportunity to strengthen the unity and cohesion of their own community. That the watchmen were recognized authorities among the slaves and that they were given responsibilities for important decisions in the life of the slave community served, no doubt, to develop their own leadership. The church provided the space for this—through limited and under the supervision of Jones and the session.[48]

The discipline which the watchmen exercised among the blacks also furnished an opportunity for giving order to this community. This was what white masters wanted, but the opportunity could also be taken by the blacks to strengthen their own solidarity. If the watchmen helped to discipline those who stole, they were not simply doing the work of the whites, but they were insisting that there was a need for moral standards among their people to keep them from self-contempt and further degradation. If the watchmen sought to solve differences among the blacks and to strengthen slave marriages, they were not simply attempting to provide the order and harmony whites desired among their laborers, but were seeking to build a more coherent black community. The discipline of the church thus reflected the ambiguity inherent in the position of these black leaders: their work helped to strengthen both the control of the whites and the ability of the blacks to resist the degradations and ideological foundations of white authority.[49]

V

During the year of 1841, Charles Jones spent forty-two such Sundays going from station to station, preaching and teaching the blacks of Liberty County. The size of his congregations and Sabbath school classes varied throughout the year and from station to station but ranged from 100 to 400 slaves. In a majority of the services no white person was present but Jones himself.[50]

Jones often lamented the large number of slaves who did not attend any of the services. "There are large numbers," he would write the next year, "that seldom or never go to the house of

God." Some, he noted, would not go "even after strong and repeated efforts to induce them to do so." Others worshipped only sporadically, and in disappointment he would admit that there were "individuals whom I have never seen at church at any time; and to a few I am not even known by sight." There were a variety of reasons, Jones believed, for this poor attendance: the distance that had to be walked from plantations to stations, age and infirmity, indolence, poor clothing, the wish to visit friends or to conduct business, and the *"strolling* about the fields and swamps and woods with their dogs, after more honest people have gone to church, and sometimes commit depredations upon cattle and hogs and sheep." "But the great reason" was "indifference to religion," and only God could provide an answer to the central issue: "Were the spirit of the Lord abroad amongst us with his convicting, converting and sanctifying influences, all other causes for the neglect of His worship in His sanctuaries would lose their power." It is not unusual, however, for preachers to complain about the size of their congregations. If one takes into account that the same individuals were not always present at each station, Jones no doubt preached to over two thousand slaves during the course of a year. His work evidently met with a significant degree of approval among many of the blacks of Liberty County. In 1844 Jones estimated, using the county tax returns, that over fifty percent of the adult slaves in Liberty County were church members.[51]

Writing in 1845, he evaluated the changes that had occurred in the slave population:

> The *general character of the Negroes,* comparing the present with the past, *is much improved.* Running away, theft, lewdness, profane swearing and filthy conversation: quarrelling, and fighting, witchcraft, Sabbath-breaking, drunkenness, violations of the marriage contract, idleness and indifference to their own comfort, and infidelity in work, have all diminished. Their appearance and manners are changed for the better. Greater numbers attend the house of God. In respect to religious knowledge, they are not the same people. . . .

There was more than a hint of propaganda in these words. They were, after all, written to convince white masters of the benefits that religious instruction brought to their slaves. And Jones was not above exaggerating his own accomplishments in spite of his piety! Still, there was truth to what he said. Visitors noted the change. Owners remarked on the improvements. And the church records indicated fewer disciplinary charges against the blacks. One planter wrote to Jones that there had been "a decided improvement in the morals and conduct of the people generally—there have not been as many riots, and thefts, and disorderly conduct, which required the interference of the whites as formerly."[52]

On the other side, however, it was clear that from the planters' perspective there was still "much wrong" among the blacks "to be regretted," and "much room for improvement." If fifty percent of the adult slaves were members of the church, fifty percent were not. There was still much that was called "disorderly conduct" among the blacks. Even church members were found who resisted the submission taught carefully at the Sabbath stations: they killed pigs in the woods, ran away, got drunk, cursed, and left husbands or wives. There was still much "witchcraft," though not so much among church members. Frizzled chickens were still kept, charms were regarded with awe, root doctors made their potions and medicines, and sacred images from a distant past were carved.[53]

From the white perspective, the work was thus a success—though a limited success with room for improvement. The gospel had been preached and submission had been taught. The moral character of the black community had been improved, at least according to white perceptions.

For the blacks, the work of Jones was no doubt regarded with mixed emotions. It was certainly clear to them that much of what he did and taught was part of the whites' attempt to keep them in submission. The fact that some blacks had clearly seen through his earlier sermon on Onesimus and that others refused to accept Jones as their preacher because he was a slaveholder and "his people have to work as well as we" showed that they were not unaware of what he was about. The question must then be asked: Why did so many come to hear him preach or respond to his labors? They knew he was a white preacher to black slaves, that even if he did not dwell on their duties, his work was intended to undergird and reinforce their slavery. Part of the answer, no doubt, can be found in his kindness. He was a man who, in many ways, gave himself to them. He was benevolent and paternal and through him many learned of a gospel that lifted their spirits beyond the cruel realities of their slavery and gave them courage in the midst of their bondage. But more important than Jones' support of slavery (blacks had no reason to expect a white planter and preacher to do otherwise), or his benevolence in the midst of it, was the fact that his work provided the blacks of Liberty County some free space of their own. Although Jones had moved into the pulpit that had once been filled by publicly acknowledged black preachers, he had the advantage of strong white support that felt little need to interfere, and therefore gave blacks, ironically enough, an important opportunity to strengthen their community with a minimum of white supervision.

When the Liberty County planter quoted above had congratulated Jones that there was now less need for "the interference of the whites as formerly" in the affairs of blacks, he was expressing relief from what he regarded as a burden. For the blacks, on the other hand, to gain less "interference" from the whites was a significant step in their struggle for some free space in the midst of slavery. And the blacks knew how to use Jones for this purpose! "Sir," said an old black man with tears in his eyes, "it is the Gospel that we ignorant and wicked people need. If you will give us the Gospel, it will do more for the obedience of servants and the peace of the community than all your guards and guns and bayonets."[54] They were words that Jones cherished. And they were words that the blacks of Liberty County hoped would help remove some of the guards and guns and bayonets of the whites.

4

A Plantation Pastor

I

Dear Mr. Mallard:
If it is agreeable and convenient, I will preach for your people on
Wednesday evening next.

RESPECTFULLY AND TRULY,
YOUR FRIEND,
C. C. J.

Standing in the parlor of the Mallard plantation house, Charles
Jones looked around. It was a large but unpretentious room
papered in a pattern of curious figures. Light from candles and
the wide fireplace danced off the room's two windows and revealed black slaves gathered for a plantation meeting. There was
Maum Willoughby, the cook, whose husband Dublin lived on a
nearby plantation. There was Henry and his wife Katy; Pompey
and his wife Milly; Harry, the best carpenter in the county; Dick,
Biffs, and Billy; Grace, who was married to Billy on Mr. Walthour's place and was always having trouble with him; "Daddy
Jack," the confirmed bachelor; Peter, the Mallard's houseservant;

as well as other blacks whom Jones did not know. Some were
seated on crude chairs or benches brought from their cabins
while others stood at the open door that led to the porch. Many
were weary from the day's labors in rice and cotton fields, and
sleep would steal over some before the evening services were
over. Yet, in spite of the fatigue, they had come to hear Jones,
who that evening had ridden over seven miles to meet with these
his "black parishioners."[1]

As Jones looked at the slaves gathered around him, he knew
that, while the Sabbath services accomplished much, "the people
absolutely required more." They needed to be visited and
preached to and instructed where they lived. They needed, just
as their white owners needed, their minister to perform the duties of a pastor. Not only that, Jones knew that he needed to visit
them if he were going to know the actual "extent of his field," its
destitutions, and the moral and religious condition of the people.
Such visitation would allow his sermons to have a "more direct
and personal application," his pastoral relationships a "more
familiar and intimate" quality, and his influence a "more extended and powerfull" authority. Above all, however, his visits
would convince the slaves of his sincerity.[2]

Jones, as was his custom, had written Thomas Mallard asking
for permission to visit his plantation. (No plantation meeting was
held or visitation undertaken without the knowledge and consent
of the owner.) Mr. Mallard had immediately given a favorable
response. A selectman and deacon at the Midway Church, Mallard had long been a supporter of Jones' missionary efforts. Now,
when he had received Jones' note, he had made arrangements for
the plantation meeting, setting the exact time and place.[3]

Because the meeting was held on a weekday night after the
slaves had finished a full day's labor, only slaves from the Mallard
plantation were allowed to attend. This was a rule Jones thought
important in order to maintain the support of the planters. He
himself never gave "any notice whatever to the negroes on other
plantations, or on the Sabbath, that meetings will be held during
the week on such and such plantations." Such a rule helped to

insure order among the slaves and avoided the appearance of a dangerous nighttime meeting. "It is a household affair altogether," wrote Jones, "and the people are little disposed to embrace such an assembly for bad purposes. If any of them wish to do evil on the plantation, they can choose another night and another occasion just as conveniently." In 1845 Jones would be able to report to the planters of Liberty County that of "some hundreds of meetings held on plantations at night, there never has occurred a single instance of riot, of theft, or unruly conduct, within my own knowledge, nor have I ever heard a complaint of any such thing. . . ."[4]

Thomas Mallard had arranged for the meeting to take place in his parlor. This was not a particularly unusual procedure and Jones had found that it had both advantages and disadvantages. It was more comfortable than meeting in the "houses of the people which are generally too small, or in plantation houses [buildings] of one kind and another which are open, cold and uncomfortable." On the other hand, meeting in the white owner's house, as in the white owner's church, left the blacks "not sufficiently at home to be at ease." Blacks wanted some free space, some place they could claim for their own, for their place of worship. This had been one of the reasons Jones had established the stations as a place for the Sabbath services. In seeking to deal with this same issue for the plantation meetings, Jones had asked the planters to build chapels or special rooms for the slaves' worship, not only when he visited, but regularly during the week. Time and again he had stressed the importance of such a place and had taught that its provision was a Christian duty of white owners. His appeals, however, were to little avail, and the neat chapel at Montevideo with its belfry and bell was one of the few built in Liberty County.[5]

When Jones had entered the Mallard parlor, he had immediately noticed some slaves who never attended the Sabbath services. Among these were "worldly persons" and even church members who were habitually absent from "the house of God." But there were others—the aged and the infirm—who were una-

ble to make the short trip from the Mallard plantation to the
Midway station. Jones felt a special obligation to all of these who
were "strangers to the house of the Lord," and much of his
pastoral visitation would be aimed at reaching them.[6]

The worship service was similar to the Sunday morning service, except that the congregation was questioned on the content
of his sermon. The service began with singing that drew to the
parlor all who had not already come in. Thomas Mallard prayed
and read the Scripture lesson to his slaves; there was another
hymn and then Jones preached. Following a closing prayer and
hymn, the slaves were dismissed. A few inquirers and those under
"serious impressions" remained behind. Jones spoke to them
about their religious lives, gave counsel, "administered re-
proofs," and settled any divisions among them.[7]

When the last of the black congregation had left the Mallard's house, Jones went out to visit among the slave cabins.
The plantation buildings which he passed were laid out so
that everything, as far as possible, was under Thomas Mallard's eye as he looked from his front door. There was a yellow clay smokehouse on the right across from the plantation
kitchen. Just beyond the front yard were the cotton storage
houses. A horse gin stood silently waiting another day for its
rattling chain to turn hickory rollers and separate the cotton
from the seed. Beyond the stables and carriage house, stretch-
ing to the left and in front, were the slave quarters. They
were two-room cabins constructed of sawed lumber loosely
covered with cypress clapboards so that "only the thickness of
a single board kept out the winter's air and cold." Around the
cabins were the small gardens of the slaves with their chicken
coops, pig pens, rice ricks, and little storage houses. Here
Jones entered the cabins to visit the aged and sick. A lone
candle and the fire from a clay hearth lit each dwelling. The
sick lay on crude beds whose mattresses were made of the
gray moss from the surrounding swamps. Standing beside
these beds, Jones reminded the black slaves of the gracious
promises of the gospel, asked them if they put their trust in

Jesus, and offered a prayer for their health and salvation. "Who can estimate," Jones would later write,

the calm, sanctifying, and saving influences of such visits both upon the pastor and the people? They necessarily lead to exposure of health; they call for self-denial, perseverance, patience, and faith. The pastor will meet with some rough and barren spots, and encounter tardiness, indifference, heaviness of eyes and inattention—yea, many things to depress and to discourage: but he must not mind them; he must pray for more faith, and more love, and more zeal; he must not dwell upon the dark side, but upon the side made bright by heavenly and precious promises, and encourage himself in the Lord his God and vigorously press on; and in due time he shall reap if he faints not.[8]

II

Jones had found from the first that one of the peculiarities of being a pastor to black slaves was that a great deal of his pastoral efforts in their behalf had to be directed toward their white owners. Because masters had control over every aspect of their slaves' lives, Jones had to influence the masters if he hoped to minister to the slaves. For this reason he sought through his personal visitations on the plantations and through his sermons, publications, and correspondence to shape the conscience of the slaveholders; he endeavored to persuade them of their responsibilities both to provide religious instruction and to administer "just and equal" treatment on the plantations. His work would play an important role in helping white southerners internalize a paternalistic ethos.

When Jones had begun his missionary efforts, he had found many whites hostile or, at best, indifferent to his labors and concerns. Not only had it been a new work in a sensitive area, but many had feared the slaves' response to the gospel and the possibilities of dangerous religious assemblies. In addition, the growing abolitionist movement had caused increasing anxiety among white slaveholders—not a few of whom had expressed their fears and objections "in no measured terms" toward Jones and his plans for religious instruction.[9]

Jones had seen in 1835 the excitement the abolitionists could cause in a southern community. In that year he had traveled to Charleston, South Carolina, to attend a presbytery meeting and to preach to both black and white Presbyterians in the city. While there, he discovered that the American Anti-Slavery Society had been mailing abolitionist literature to southern leaders. An angry mob had entered the United States Post Office in Charleston, seized the anti-slavery mail, and burned it in the public square. In a letter to his wife, he had written that the "greatest excitement here has been and now is, on the Abolition question, and sorry am I to inform you that the cause of Religious Instruction has been most seriously injured. . . . Nothing can be attempted until the fever cools." Henry L. Pinckney, a member of an important Charleston family, informed Jones of a "strong opposition to Religious Instruction" and told him that "all who do anything for Negroes were in a 'ticklish' situation." Jones had responded that his friends had never accused him of rashness in his operations, and "that it was best in periods of excitement to yield to the storm, until it was passed."[10] He would later watch with satisfaction the white ministers of Charleston turn, with a zeal unequalled in any other southern city, to the religious instruction of slaves.

This anti-slavery furor in the 1830's and its continuing agitation had an important influence on Jones as he sought to be a pastor to black slaves. On the one hand, it meant he had to overcome the growing paranoia of southern whites in the face of the increasing strength of the abolitionists. He had to convince the slaveowners what he was about as a pastor was not a threat to the South's "peculiar institution." On the other hand, he had to respond to the abolitionists' criticism of slavery by stressing the need of masters to care for not only the spiritual but also the physical welfare of their slaves. Within this context, he attempted to influence the masters by appealing to both their self-interest and to the Bible.[11]

Standing in the Old School Presbyterian tradition, Jones was a realist who believed in the depravity of the human heart: "the *power* of the principle of *self-interest,*" Jones had told the graduating class at Columbia Seminary in 1837, is "the *'primum mobile'* of human action." A Calvinistic understanding of sin was not, however, the only reason Jones viewed human motivation in terms of self-interest. He had seen how slavery itself kept the evil side of the human heart before the community: there were too many instances of cruelty and the role of power in human affairs was clearly before the southern eye in black and white. Slave scenes limited a person's ability to appeal to the higher motivation of liberty, equality, and self-sacrifice for the neighbor. Both Christian insight and economic system, therefore, led Jones to stress the self-interest of the masters as he sought to influence them in behalf of the slaves.[12]

The heart of Jones' argument for self-interest was based upon the axiom that "virtue is more profitable than vice." If a planter sought to exercise his "duties" toward his slaves with integrity, if he were virtuous and honorable, his plantation profits would increase and the quality of life between owner and owned would be improved. Cotton would be picked and rice harvested with less loss of time, less trouble, and fewer disciplinary problems. The master would be "measurably relieved from perpetual watching, from fault-finding and threatening and heart-sickening severity"; and he could "begin at least to govern somewhat by the law of love." All of this would combine to make the plantation more profitable.[13]

Human motivation, however, in Jones' understanding, was not only a result of self-interest but also a response to God's grace, and it was to this motivation that Jones made his strongest appeal for the establishment of Christian plantations. In order to minister to the black slaves of Liberty County, Jones' message to masters called for the planters to be changed in mind and heart by the introduction of the Christian faith into their own lives. "Religion will quicken the master's conscience," wrote Jones, "and before he is aware perhaps, his servants will be greatly elevated in his regards, and he will feel himself bound and willing to do more and more for them." Such a changed attitude would lead to those changes in plantation government that Jones was concerned about as a pastor to black slaves. "His interest," wrote Jones of the Christian master, "will not be the sole object of pursuit. . . . He will have an eye to the comfort, the interest of his people, and endeavor to identify their interest with his, and also to make them see and feel it to be so."[14]

III

Sitting before the fire in the Mallard parlor where slaves had gathered earlier in the evening for worship, Charles Jones talked with Thomas Mallard. It was often Jones' custom after visiting in the slave quarters to return to the plantation house for a visit with the planter and his family; it provided him an opportunity to discuss—no doubt prudently and with good southern manners—those duties of masters that he had emphasized so often in his sermons and writings. Such discussions, he felt, were an important part of his ministry to black slaves.

As Mallard and Jones sat before the fire, they very well may have discussed the week's activities and their various responsibilities as plantation owners and Christian masters. Mallard trusted and respected Jones (you had to trust a man to let him visit among your slave quarters with all of their intimations about an owner's character). Now as they talked, Mallard no doubt heard Jones express some of the concerns he had been pressing upon the planters of Liberty County.

A master's first responsibility, insisted Jones, was to provide for their slaves' salvation. Masters ought to instruct their servants in the Scriptures and give them every opportunity and encouragement to seek their salvation. That very year he had warned his fellow slaveholders: "Your responsibilities in the word and providence of God are very great. If you neglect them, a fearful account awaits you!" There were, however, many things owners could do for the spiritual welfare of their slaves. For a long time Jones had been urging planters to hold evening meetings for their slaves, read them interesting stories from the Bible, and teach them from a suitable catechism. In particular, plantation schools ought to be established for black children to teach them about the Christian faith and to help civilize them to white ways. Such schools could change the young blacks from "wild, half-clothed, boisterous" children into better behaved, "more pleasant profitable servants, and when grown better husbands and wives." It was a shame, he complained, that even in Liberty County this responsibility was neglected by planters and that the education of black children depended all too often upon the Sabbath schools.[15]

Jones knew that Mallard was conscientious about the keeping of the Sabbath day and allowed neither his "manservant, nor his maidservant, nor his cattle, nor any stranger that was within his gates" to labor on the holy day. In talking to white masters after his visits to slave quarters, Jones often noted, however, the importance of Sabbath observance. One of his constant themes was that if masters were to follow God's word, they must permit and encourage their slaves to keep the Sabbath day holy. Over and over again he had said that masters were to require no work for themselves or spend the day in recreation: masters ought to prohibit their slaves from *"all labour"* such as "planting, attending to their crops, harvesting, repairing their fences or houses, trading, washing, grinding and *all pleasures,* such as hunting and fishing and playing at games."[16]

Jones recognized that there were particular problems for slaves, as for "all labouring and mechanical classes," in regard to keeping the Sabbath day. "The Sabbath" he would report to the Liberty County planters, "is their day of rest, of recreation and enjoyment, and they are at home with their families, or abroad luxuriating in forbidden indulgences, and in freedom from occupation and care." If a planter worked his slaves so hard during the week that they had no time for themselves, or if he required his slaves to work for him on the Sabbath, then "the burden of

sin is on his shoulders." Such conduct could not be "spoken of
in terms of too severe reprobation." It called for the "attention
of the civil authorities and the severest pentalities provided in
law."[17]

IV

In seeking to minister to the slaves through an appeal to their
white masters, Jones discussed with Mallard and the other planters the question of slave discipline. During the early days of his
missionary labors when he was struggling for the support of
planters, Jones had found that it was necessary to overcome the
popular idea that religious instruction led to poor discipline
among the slaves. In his first report to the Liberty County Association, he had noted that some planters did "relax discipline as
soon as they begin to give religious instruction," while others,
hearing of such and knowing that it was folly, "discard such
instruction altogether." This situation led him to call for "strict
discipline to be continued and perfected" on the plantations,
while religious instruction was at the same time provided. Even
in the early years of his work, however, Jones was quick to point
out that strict discipline and severity were not the same thing.
Endeavoring to temper the stringency of punishment, he offered
an alternative: "The great principle to be infixed is *subordination.*
That infixed, and in general discipline is easy: that is, as easy as
it can be with people in their condition." This subordination
which was to replace severity would come, of course, with religious instruction as it taught slaves their "God-given" place in
southern society. Jones' efforts to pastor black slaves by working
for less severe punishment were thus intended at the same time
to make the slaves more easily managed and more subordinate
laborers.[18]

By the time Jones and Mallard sat talking in 1841, Jones had
strong community support for his work and was in a much more

secure position to speak out on the issues of discipline and the treatment of slaves. In that year he would write that one of the most important problems in "the moral and religious character of the Negroes," was that the *"government* to which they are subjected is *too much physical in its nature."* Appeals to the fear of punishment "should be made as seldom as possible and in the mildest form consistent with due support of authority and reformation of the transgressor." When punishments were necessary, they should be inflicted only upon those proven guilty, never "in anger, nor out of proportion to the *offence,"* with as "little resort to *corporal chastisement* as possible." Instead of physical punishments, Jones suggested that "confinement and deprivation of priviledges . . . , as well as other modes" ought to be employed.[19]

V

One of the most sensitive areas that Jones discussed with the planters as he visited was the standard of living among the slaves. His attempts to improve their physical conditions represented one of the most significant ways he sought to be a pastor to the blacks of Liberty County.

Jones insisted that the improvement of the slaves' standard of living strengthened their moral life and witnessed to the truth of the masters' religion. He was aware of the social sources of spiritual and moral character and that the environmental conditions of a community significantly shaped the lives and values of its members. "The physical improvement of the Negroes," he told the Liberty County planters, "is not only our duty, but it stands in immediate connection with their moral and religious improvement. . . ." At the same time, planters who showed an interest in their slaves' physical conditions demonstrated the truth of the Christian faith: "If you do not labor and be at some sacrifice of time and means to improve their *physical condition,* . . . if you fail to impress your people with the belief that you are really their friend, and desire their best good for this world as well as for the next, and you honestly intend to promote it, as far as it lies in your power, they cannot and will not value your instruction." If planters sought to use religion merely as a form of social control and refused because of selfish and materialistic interests to be concerned about the poor who were their responsibility, they were hypocrites and their black slaves would not be deceived:

> They themselves are indeed professors of religion, but their people behold them as covetous and grasping and driving, and as anxious after earthly goods and enjoyments as are most men of the world. Their people perceive that they are neglected in their houses, clothing, food, land to plant, opportunities of making something for themselves; that their prosperity and conveniences and comforts are passed over. Can any man, treating his servants in this manner, suppose that he will be credited in his professions, or that they will follow his advise, or delight to wait upon his instructions? . . . The true character of masters is seldom misunderstood by servants. It is better known to them than to their most intimate friends.[20]

As Jones visited among the slave quarters of Liberty County he identified six particular areas that needed reform if slaves were to have "just and equal" treatment.

It was obvious to Jones that masters needed first of all to improve the housing conditions of their slaves. Their general mode of living, he observed, was "coarse and vulgar"; their houses were frequently "small, low to the ground, blackened with smoke, often with dirt floors, and the furniture of the plainest kind. . . ." Privacy was impossible. While southern agricultural journals often warned masters about the importance of furnishing good houses for their laborers, Jones insisted that it was a religious duty masters owed their slaves. He asked masters how they expected religion or morality to thrive in squalid quarters. Poor housing resulted in poor morals—crowding two or more families in one house "scarcely large enough for one family" and mingling up "husbands and wives, children and youth" banished the "privacy and modesty essential to domestic peace and purity" and opened wide the door "to dishonesty, oppression, violence and profligacy." Every slave family on a plantation, "whether consisting of only husband and wife, or parents and children, or of *one* parent and children, should have a *house of its own, in undisputed and undisturbed possession.*" The houses should be "convenient and comfortable" and "properly partitioned off, and well ventilated, and neatly whitewashed, and sufficiently large to accomodate the families resident in them; and furnished with necessary articles for household use." Special attention needed to be paid to the welfare of the slave children and different sleeping apartments provided "for boys and girls as they become more advanced." (Following this counsel, Thomas Mallard had arranged that when the black children on his plantation were "half grown" one or two "shed-rooms" or "leantos" should be built on the back of the cabins to provide the proper privacy.)[21]

Then there was the question of clothes for slaves. How easy it was for planters to let their slaves go about in rags, a bit of this and a bit of that, an occasional old coat or dress discarded as useless by a white family. It could all be so easily justified by saying they were Africans and accustomed to going about half naked. Jones himself believed that the slaves were "exceedingly inattentive to the preservation of their clothing" because of their African traditions. It was, nevertheless, the duty of masters both to provide clothing and to require slaves to care for them. On the Mallard plantation, as was the general custom, black seamstresses made most of the clothes from homemade cloth, and one wool blanket was given each worker every alternate year.[22]

"Servants should be provided," Jones insisted, "with *abundant food,* and that wholesome and good, and as diversified as it can conveniently be made." The slaves on the Mallard plantation had corn which they ground on the plantation's hand mill as the staple of their diet. This was supplemented by sweet potatoes which were cooked in ashes or baked before the fire in the fireplace. There were greens from the garden, rice from their patches, "chickens and bacon of their own raising and curing, and fish of their own catching."[23]

Medical care was a fourth duty of masters to slaves. Any wise manager of a plantation would know that, if their slaves were provided with better houses, clothes, and food, their health would improve "and the expense of lost labor by sickness, and of physicians' bills would be saved."[24] Jones, however, went beyond a prudential care for the health of one's laborers and valuable property and insisted that it was the duty of masters to care for those who were "old and infirmed and crippled and useless" and no longer of any economic value. They were not to be put away and ignored in some little cabin in the woods where they would have to care for themselves in their weakness. The planters themselves could provide medical care following as best as they were able some practical medical book such as *Ewell's Practice.* (The most popular cure for general ailments for whites and blacks was castor oil!) If a Liberty County slave became seriously ill, Dr. Samuel Way or Dr. King could be sent for by any of the planters—and he often was.

When Jones was away at Philadelphia, his slave Cato wrote to him:

> We have had some Sickness Since Mr. Shepard last wrote you Fanny was threatened with Pleurisy for several days but is up and well again. And Negar was taken verry violently on Saturday week last. I gave oil & Blistered and poulticed and he grew So Much worse as though the pain in his Side would Cut away his breath that I could not risque to wait till day light but Sent John off to Mr. Shepard who soon as he got the word Sent Dr King who came a little before day and found him badly off and after taking a heap of blood & Enlarging the blister, gave relief Mr Shepard kept him in the house all this week and would not suffer him to come out fearing a relapse until this morning, he is now out again.[25]

But Thomas Mallard's son Robert would remember that the doctors were often sent for so late that "to send for the doctor" meant "to give up the case," and was regarded as an ominous sign.[26]

A fifth duty of masters was to refrain from overworking their slaves and to provide free time for them. In his catechism, Jones had written the following question and answer for the slaves to recite:

Q. Ought he, the master, to require them to do what they are unable to do; or what would be unlawful for them to do?
A. No.

It is the masters' duty, said Jones, "to lay upon their servants *that labour only which is just;* allow time to enjoy the comforts of life and to do something for themselves, and preserve to them *sacredly the rest of the sabbath.*"[27]

Finally, Jones believed the slaves were "entitled to a far larger portion of the avails of their labor, than they have hertofore been accustomed to receive." He also felt slaves ought to have a place for themselves and a means to earn money: "They should have opportunity to plant something for themselves, and opportunity to attend to, and to harvest their crops, and to dispose of what they raise or make for sale." Jones wanted each slave house to have "a small lot for a garden, poultry yard, apiary, and other purposes, attached to it." But also of importance was the allowance of a place for enterprising slaves to work. Beside the small plot, Jones encouraged masters to make available for their slaves "as much ground to plant for themselves during the year as they can profitably attend; and also the privilege of raising poultry and hogs; indeed every privilege and opportunity allowed them to make themselves comfortable and to accumulate money." Slaves who were allowed such privileges could be enterprising "improving their opportunities" by selling poultry, stock and produce "to the amount of thirty, fifty, and a hundred dollars."[28]

If Jones sought to minister to black slaves of Liberty County through appeals to their white masters, he also found that the slaves had their own standards and expectations. These reflected both their understanding of the "duties" of masters and their own values as they had evolved through the experience of their people. They sought, for example, to dress in a manner that demonstrated their own self-respect. That they were often ragged is not surprising given the clothes that were provided them and the demoralizing effects of slavery. What is surprising is that they often dressed well, to both the amusement and indignation of many whites, and that they did not hesitate to make demands on their paternalistic owners for clothing they felt to be proper for certain occasions such as weddings or church services. In the same manner they used their gardens to develop their spirit of independence. The slaves of Mallard, Jones, and neighboring plantations had large gardens as well as small rice fields for their own cultivation and use. By carefully tending these and by taking advantage of the opportunities for hunting and fishing, they were able not only to vary their diets but also to provide their families a certain degree of security and comfort.[29]

VI

In attempting to minister to the black slaves he visited on the plantations of Liberty County, Jones met no more difficult problem than the question of slave marriages and family life. He was aware, perhaps painfully aware, that the system of slavery made slave marriages tenuous at best. "The divine institution of marriage," he wrote in 1841, "depends for its perpetuity, sacredness, and value, largely upon the protection given it by the law of the land." Yet, he said, "Negro marriages are neither recognized nor protected by law." Jones felt that because slave marriages were not protected by law the whole fabric of southern society was threatened, for marriage was a divine institution, ordained of God, and first in order of time and importance in human relationships. If the institution of marriage were threatened, the whole society was threatened.[30]

It was clear to Jones—it would have been hard, of course, for it not to be clear—that slave marriages were not secure because of the legal status of slaves as chattel property. Jones charged that slave families "are and may be divided for improper conduct on the part of either husband or wife, or by necessity, as in cases of the death of owners, division of estates, debt, sale, or removals, for they are subject to all the changes and vicissitudes of *property.* " The non-existence of legal marriage among slaves and the property rights of owners in the slave's person resulted in slave marriages that were "contracts of convenience, profit or pleasure, that may be entered into and dissolved at the will of the parties, and that without heinous sin, or the injury of the property or interests of any one." Separations took place for what Jones considered to be the most shallow of reasons: "protracted sickness, want of industrious habits, of congeniality of disposition, or disparity of age. . . ."[31]

The situation in regard to slave marriages accentuated Jones' fundamental problem as he sought to be a pastor to black slaves: he was seeking to work within a cruel and unjust economic and social system undergirded and strengthened by the churches in the South. The possibility of an encounter between Christianity and slavery was thus reduced to the sphere of personal relationships. Jones could visit individual planters, speak and write of their personal duties to God and "servants," and seek to influence them through his own personal example, but he could not and would not seek a radical change of the system. The closest he came to challenging the system, however, was in regard to slave marriages. So fundamental was marriage to his understanding of the divine order of society that he could not avoid some tension with a system that allowed slave marriages to be arbitarily broken by owners. In spite of the magnitude of the problems, Jones hoped that changes could take place in regard to slave marriages. He stressed that masters had two duties: to encourage slave marriages and to keep slave families together.

"Owners should encourage early marriages, and take an interest in seeing that the connections which their people form are suitable and promising in character," wrote Jones. Encouragement, however, did not mean coercion, and Jones worked to limit the authority of the planters while he sought their support. "Marriages contracted from necessity; too frequently result in misery, or immorality, or in separation." Slaves ought to have "the freedom of choice of their affections" for "they are a people having their preferences as well as others." Asked Jones: "Can that love which is the foundation and essence of the marriage state, be forced?" He thought not.[32]

In an effort to enlarge the slaves' role on the choice of a spouse, Jones argued that the marriage partners should not of necessity be confined to a single plantation. The issue resolved around what the slave wanted: "if the preference be to someone abroad" and there were *"no other* objections" excepting the planters' "desire for marriages upon their own plantations, then the union should not be prevented." Such a practice meant some freedom of choice for the blacks, but at the same time it emphasized their bondage. There was, for example, Thomas Mallard's cook Maum Willoughby who was married to Dublin, a slave from another plantation. They could see each other only on the weekend. Every Saturday evening he would join other black men travelling the roads of Liberty County to their "wife houses." He would bring a bag of his soiled clothes for his wife to wash as well as any "good thing" he could manage to collect during the week for his family. This arrangement was not unusual in Liberty County. On the Mallard plantation there were, in addition to Maum Willoughby and Dublin, at least two other marriages with slaves of other plantations: Grace was married to Billy on Mr. Walthour's plantation, and Harry was married to a woman on another nearby plantation.[33]

White owners were clearly the greatest threat to slave families. "They should *not separate,"* declared Jones, *"nor allow separation of husband and wife, unless for causes lawful before God."* The problem that Jones had to confront here as elsewhere was the planters' unlimited authority over the lives of their slaves. In regard to slave marriages, what he attempted to do was to set God's law over against the masters' legal rights. It was a question of obedience to God. If masters wished to use the Bible for a pro-slavery argument, then they must be obedient to the Scriptures and honor the marriage relationships of their slaves. "Does an owner presume to contract or annul the marriage of his servants at his pleasure and for his own interest and convenience or by any of his own arbitrary regulations?" asked Jones. If so, the judgment of God awaits the master: "He shall answer to Him, who hath said, 'What therefore God hath joined together let no man put asunder.' "[34]

Plantation masters were not to break up marriages because of "the want of congenial dispositions," or because of quarrelling or violence between the partners. "The distance at which they live apart," "dishonest character or conduct," or disrespect of "the peace or arrangement" on the plantation were not justifiable reasons for separation—although this list indicates some of the arguments Jones encountered. Most important of all, however, Jones insisted masters should not "separate husband and wife either by sale or purchase."[35]

Even in Liberty County, however, where both the white and black populations were relatively stable, Jones' admonitions in regard to slave families were not always carefully followed. In 1839 several white families moved to Florida, taking their slaves with them. For those slaves whose husbands or wives lived on another plantation, this meant separation and the break-up of their families. There was Judy, the slave of Mr. Bacon, whose husband had been carried by his owner to Quincy, Florida. And there was Henry: his wife had been taken to Florida and he asked the session at Midway if he were free to marry again. Mr. Stacy and Mr. Cassels were instructed to investigate the probability of her return. If there were no prospect, they were to say to Henry "that he *may marry another woman,* but if she will *probably return* he must not *marry again.*" Three months later it was reported that it was very doubtful that she would ever come back to her home in Liberty County. And there were others: Biner and Warwick and John. Not many, perhaps, if one measures such things by statistics. But some things cannot be measured.[36]

There were some owners who sought to keep slave families together, even when it meant an economic loss for them. When Harry Steven's wife and children were freed by their owner in order to be sent to Liberia, Thomas Mallard, Steven's master, freed him with some financial support from other planters. And when Jones himself had a young slave woman run away, he sold her and her parents and younger brothers and sisters together as a family.[37]

It was not, of course, white masters who made the most strenuous efforts to keep slave families together; it was the slaves themselves. In spite of their vulnerability as chattel property, they struggled to strengthen their family ties and to develop a strong sense of family identification. At least for those who were church members, this meant there were expectations of fidelity between the marriage partners. When Harry, the slave of Thomas Mallard, found that his wife had committed adultery, he asked for and was granted a divorce from her by the session at Midway. Thirteen years later, Henry, another slave of Mallard's, brought charges against his wife Katy. He was released from her having proved her "unfaithfulness to him." Several years later, Susan, one of the Jones' houseservants, brought charges of unfaithfulness against her husband Andrew and was granted a divorce from him by the Midway session. In all of this, there were expectations on the part of black husbands and wives that their spouses would be faithful. Robert Mallard would remember that, among the slaves of Liberty County, marriages were regarded as sacred and the "obligations as commonly observed as among the same class anywhere." Indeed, long and faithful marriages were the rule rather than the exception among the black members of Midway, and the church discipline that was brought against those who were unfaithful was a means of sanctioning and reinforcing those expectations of fidelity.[38]

The evidence of long marriages among Liberty County blacks and their concern to strengthen their family ties can be seen in the very names they gave their children. On the Jones plantations there were a number of black families that streched over several generations: Robin was named after his grandfather "Daddy Robin;" Niger I had his son Niger II and his grandson Niger III named after him; Sam had a son Sam and saw his granddaughter Tenah give birth to a daughter who was not only his but also Niger I's great-granddaughter—and the child was named after her grandmother Lucy. There was Andrew and his son Andrew, Gilbert and his son Gilbert, and a whole host of Kates named after grandmothers and mothers and aunts. Among the blacks at Montevideo and the surrounding plantations of Liberty County, there was as bewildering a network of extended family relations as among the whites. They sent their love and their "howdies" to each other in the letters that the whites wrote to one another and no doubt communicated with each other frequently through their own "grapevine."[39]

Jones sought to strenghen these family ties through his preaching to the blacks and through his writings and discussions on the duties of masters. He preached in 1841 to his black congregation at the Newport station a series of sermons on marriage. These homilies dealt with the nature of marriage and the duties of husbands and wives. They were a great success in attracting large numbers of blacks to the services so that "in order to accomodate the people, the lower floor was appropriated to married persons and the gallery to single persons." The themes were those he had been teaching in his catechism about marriage: a man was to have only one wife, a woman only one husband; before marriage a person was to be "pure and virtuous," after marriage faithful and loving; marriage was to be based on love—a person ought not to marry unless the love for the partner were greater than love for father, mother, brother or sister.[40]

Jones encouraged the blacks to be married by a "minister, or some other lawful person." Prior to his ministry, marriages among slaves in Liberty County were seldom performed by an ordained minister. Many, no doubt, had been solemnized by the old practice of the couple simply jumping across a broomstick together. Once Jones began his work, however, he performed many marriages among the slaves of Liberty County:

> As soon as the parties were ready I entered the house: they presented themselves; the ceremony was performed, accompanied with plain remarks on the nature, design and duties of the marriage state. When the individuals were seated, I advanced and

addressed a few words of congratulations to them, and then bidding the company good evening, took my leave.[41]

There was, for example, the marriage of William to Kate. William was the slave of Charles Jones, Jr., who was living in Savannah, and Kate was the slave of Susan Cumming, the sister of Charles Jones, Sr. They were to be married on Saturday evening, but much to William's disappointment his father had failed to get him his coat in time, and the wedding was postponed until the next morning when the couple appeared at Montevideo to be married. "We went down" wrote Mrs. Jones to her son, "and had them brought into the parlor—bride and bridesmaid in *swiss muslins* with white wreaths on their heads, Sam and William in broadcloth and white gloves. A number of witnesses crowded in. The nuptials being over, I invited the bridal party to retire to the kitchen and partake of a hot breakfast. It was a freezing, shivering morning, and I thought that they had displayed a great deal of principle in coming over to be married in the proper manner." Sam, who evidently "gave the bride away," was Kate's uncle; and Flora, one of the bridesmaids, was a cousin. Several years later, when Kate's cousin Tenah was married to the third generation Niger, it was another impressive wedding. "I have been getting her dress ready," wrote Mrs. Jones. "Her heart was set upon a swiss muslin, so I gave her one. She has been a good, faithful servant to me and always a kind nurse to my children, so I felt she was entitled to a nice dress." Not only Tenah's owner but also her mother Lucy had a part in the preparations: "Being labor-saving and self-sparing in her notions, . . . she preferred to buy bread and cake rather than 'bother with the making.' "[42]

Probably following the more usual form for the wedding services of Liberty County blacks was the marriage of Elvira. It came in the closing days of slavery, shortly after the death of Jones, and no doubt revealed the wedding service as it had evolved among blacks during the time of Jones' ministry. Henry, one of the black watchmen, performed the service. Mrs. Jones, feeling the press of the war years, brought as a wedding gift some "substantials

and a syrup cake and a pone." She found the slave cabin arranged
with "bridal decorations":

> Wreaths of china brier were festooned over the doors and
> around the room, and on the mantelpiece stood two bottles filled
> with large bunches of dogwood flowers. *Flora* was one of the
> bridesmaids, and Tom one of the groomsmen.[43]

There was a festive air about these wedding celebrations, yet
they carried a hidden intensity with their gathered family and
friends, with their dogwood blossoms and demands for the
proper clothes. There was a haunting awareness, even an intensity of consciousness, that these slave marriages opened black
men and women not only to the possibilities of new joy but also
new griefs and sorrows. William and Kate's marriage would be
seriously threatened when Charles Jones, Jr., moved his family
away from Liberty County, and it would be only through William's persistent pleading with his master that Kate and her children would be purchased so that the marriage and family could
be kept together. Not all, however, would end so happily, and,
as we shall later see, Charles Jones, pastor to plantation slaves,
would be an intimate part of two of these tragedies.[44]

Slave marriages thus exposed the vulnerability of blacks to the
power of whites and revealed the amazing courage of men and
women who took the risk of loving those who could be sold away.
This courage came in part, and it is an astonishing irony, from
a faith nurtured by Charles Jones and other white slaveholders
and ministers. That black men and women could receive the
message of the gospel from white oppressors, and in light of their
own history and experience transform it into a great source of
faith and courage, would become perhaps the most astounding
chapter in the history of American religious life.

T W O

THE CITY

5

The Capital of the South

I

In the spring of 1845, Charles C. Jones left the lonely rice and cotton plantations of Liberty County for Charleston, South Carolina, the "Capital of the South." Jones was going to Charleston to attend an important meeting that had been called by a number of prominent members of the city to stimulate interest in the religious welfare of black slaves.

Sailing from Savannah, Jones' ship entered Charleston Harbor. The strong rich smell of the marsh blended with the fresh sea breezes. To the left lay Morris Island with its palmettos and high white dunes. Fort Sumter, a great pentagon of masonry built upon a reef to guard the harbor entrance, was straight ahead. Above the fort flew the Stars and Stripes, while in the distance was the outline of Charleston. The city stood on a peninsula between two rivers, and proud Charlestonians liked to say—half in earnest, half in jest—that it was here that the Ashley and the Cooper Rivers came together to form the Atlantic Ocean.

The city that Jones saw before him, however, was no longer the

largest or the richest in the South. During the years that Jones
had been laboring among the slaves of Liberty County, Charleston had shown little growth. In a few months a former resident
of the city, now living in New Orleans, would write, "When the
Crescent City consisted of a few huts on the low lands of the
Mississippi, her sister of the Palmetto State was reveling in the
riches of foreign commerce, and in all affluence and property.
But now the vision is changed. The noble city on the banks of the
Cooper and Ashley looks back to the past with lingering regret"
as the Louisiana port moves ahead.[1]

Jones knew that this decline was not because the citizens of
Charleston had not also tried to move ahead. Not at all! They had
built a railroad to Augusta which at the time was the longest in
the world. They had sought markets in the Ohio Valley and
commercial ties with Europe. But cotton had moved West across
the mountains, closer to Mobile and New Orleans, so that
Charleston was no longer the commercial center of the South.
During the years ahead, its economic life would be marked by
stagnation if not decay.[2]

Still, Charleston was Charleston. If it had lost its commercial
power, it had been able to maintain its claim to the title "Capital
of the South" through its cultural and political leadership. Jones
could clearly see the proud symbols of the city's influence as his
ship moved through the harbor toward the Cooper River. Out-
lined against church steeples rising above tree tops, stately
homes rimmed the city. At the tip of the peninsula, White Point
Gardens spread seaward until the Battery challenged the tide
with her high stone wall. Here was the most prestigious neighborhood in the South, for in these elegant homes overlooking the
blue bay lived Ravenels and Pinckneys, Alstons and DeSaussures,
Legares and Rhetts. Here was an established aristocracy whose
ways and manners were closely watched and carefully emulated
by a class-conscious South.[3]

The city was perhaps at the height of her political power as
Jones' ship moved toward her. Political leadership in the South
had shifted from Virginia to South Carolina: John C. Calhoun,

Charleston's adopted son, defended the South with the logic and drive of a Scotch-Irish frontiersman seduced by the images of aristocracy, while Robert Barnwell Rhett and his "fire-eating" friends were helping to pave the way for South Carolina and the South to secede from the Union.[4]

As the ship came to her mooring at Adger's wharf, Jones could see before him the beauty of Charleston that made the city both a favorite resort of planters and a powerful image in the minds of southern whites. It was springtime in Charleston and Jones' route to the Adger home where he was staying led him through the heart of the city. Riding down East Bay, which ran parallel to the Cooper River, Jones saw a mass of springtime color: red azaleas grew thick and tall under white dogwood, and blue wisteria climbed over garden walls, while the scent of the wisteria and tea olive perfumed the air, giving a seductive sensation of ease and leisure. Turning off East Bay onto Broad Street, Jones passed a neat row of law offices—there was Pettigru, King, and DeSaussure and the brokerage firms of Hume, DeSaussure, and Porcher which handled among other "things" the sale of black slaves.[5]

II

At the corner of Broad and Meeting Streets stood St. Michael's Episcopal Church. Her tall steeple marked the heart of Charleston and her bells sounded the passing time for the city. To be a member of St. Michael's was a mark of great distinction and, it was said by some, to be buried in St. Michael's old flower-covered cemetery was better than being alive and forced to live in another city. All was not well, however, at St. Michael's. The minister, Paul Trapier, had come under the influence of the Tractarians and the Oxford Movement of the Anglican Church. Trapier's High Church views were not well received by many in the congregation and had alienated him from the Protestant ministers of the city. Already Daniel Ravenel, a life-long member of St. Michael's, had left the church and had with others revived the French Huguenot Church. They had built a new building on the site of the old. It was only a few doors from another Episcopal Church, St. Philips, whose ancient cemetery would in a few short years be receiving the remains of John C. Calhoun to lie in rest with other distinguished South Carolinians.[6]

In contrast to the few scattered churches of Liberty County, Jones could see as he rode past St. Michael's and turned north on Meeting Street that Charleston was clearly a city full of churches. Back to his left on Meeting Street could be seen the First (Scots) Presbyterian Church. This church with its twin towers and cupolas had maintained close ties with the Scottish Kirk. Her ministers all came from Scotland, and Dr. John Forrest who now served there was no exception. A native of Edinburg, he had graduated from its university and still maintained his membership in the Scottish Presbytery.[7]

The First Scots Church had grown out of the Old Congregational Church which Jones now passed on his way down Meeting Street. This church had been originally known as "The White Meeting House" (from which Meeting Street took its name) and was now called the Circular Congregational Church because of its unusual shape. Just as the Scots Church drew her ministers from Scotland, so the Circular Church drew hers from New England. Dr. Ruben Post, the present pastor, was from Vermont, while his predecessor Benjamin Morgan Palmer was from a Massachusetts family. It had been during Dr. Palmer's pastorate that the congregation had divided and the Unitarian Church on Archdale Street organized. Dr. Samuel Gilman, another New Englander, now served as pastor of this Unitarian Church in the "Capital of the South." Gilman was a poet, of sorts, and would write for his alma mater "Fair Harvard."

As Jones rode further down Meeting Street he could see still more Charleston churches. A short distance from the Circular Church, on a narrow street leading off to the right, stood the Cumberland Methodist Church. This church represented both the troubles and the successes that Methodism had enjoyed in Charleston. Forty years before Jones rode by the church there had been frequent riots before it as unruly mobs had sought to disrupt the Methodist services. On one occasion the minister had been attacked and held under a water pump until rescued by friends. The problem was that for years the Methodists of Charleston had been made up almost entirely of blacks. The Annual Report of 1815 had listed 282 whites and 3,793 blacks. There had been claims that black Methodists had been involved in the Denmark Vesey planned insurrection, and several schisms had grown out of racial problems among the already weak Methodist churches of the city. Now, however, as Jones rode down Meeting Street, he could see a prosperous and respected Cumberland Methodist Church. The primary reason for this was the work of William Capers, who was presently serving as pastor of the church. Capers was editor of the *Southern Christian Advocate* and would soon be elected Bishop of the newly organized Methodist Episcopal Church, South. A man after Jones' own heart, Capers had labored long and hard for the religious welfare of the black slaves of the South and was perhaps the only man in the country equal to Jones in the leadership he had provided for this cause.[9]

Passing Hazel Street, Jones could see St. Mary's Roman Catholic Church off to the left. The parent church of the Roman Catholic Diocese of the Carolinas and Georgia, St. Mary's had seen her numbers swell in 1793 when the Marquis de Grasse with 100 white passengers and 14 slaves had escaped St. Domingo during a slave insurrection. The following years had brought other refugees and French had become the language of the congregation. At the turn of the century St. Mary's had been at the center of a controversy that had shaken the young and relatively weak American Catholic Church. The controversy had been between lay trustee control of the congregation and the authority of the hierarchy. Now, however, that aberration had ended and St. Mary's was under the firm control of the Reverend P. N. Lynch who would soon become the third Bishop of Charleston. Lynch would follow John England who, as Bishop of Charleston, had become the leader of the American hierarchy.[10]

Directly across Hazel Street from St. Mary's was Beth Elohim Synagogue. Just as St. Mary's could claim to be the parent church of the Carolinas and Georgia, so Beth Elohim could claim to be the parent of Reformed Synagogues in America. The membership of Beth Elohim included many wealthy merchants who, like the Tobias family, were well received by Charleston society.[11]

Jones was now moving toward Charleston Neck, a suburb on the city's only land boundary. The Neck was a combination of great affluence and wretched poverty. Magnificent homes could be seen lining the streets, but shacks and shanties could be found as well. Jones approached a tree-lined park. Immediately beyond it was the Joseph Manigault mansion. At the head of the park, about one half block back from Meeting Street, stood the Second Presbyterian Church. With the green lawn, the colonnade of trees and blooming azaleas of the park, the large white-columned church touched deep places in a southern heart. The pastor, Thomas Smyth, a fiery Irishman from Belfast, had recently published several heavy volumes attacking the Oxford Movement and the "claims of prelacy," winning for himself a doctorate from Princeton and the praise of British evangelicals.[12]

Smyth was also the son-in-law of James Adger, whose home Jones was now quickly approaching. While his route from Adger's Wharf to the Adger home had taken him past many of Charleston's churches, there were others that had been beyond his view. Back in the heart of the old city, not too far from Adger's Wharf, stood the First Baptist Church—a large classical building tucked away on narrow Church Street. The first of what would later be a multitude of Baptist churches in the South, this was by far the largest and most influential of the three Baptist churches in the city. Many members of old Charleston families had been immersed in the waters of the baptistry on Church Street, and while they were not among the first families of Charleston, they were respected citizens of the city.[13]

Another church hidden from Jones' view was St. John's Lutheran Church. This church would be of special interest to Jones, for the pastor, Dr. John Bachman, was one of those who had joined together to call the meeting on the religious welfare of the black slaves which Jones had come to the city to attend. Bachman was from Philadelphia and held a Ph.D. from the University of Berlin. He was both the most influential leader of the Lutheran Church in the South and a distinguished scientist. Co-author with John J. Audubon of the monumental *Quadrupeds of North America,* he was perhaps the most outstanding naturalist in the country. In a few short months he would begin to turn his considerable theological and scientific talents to the defense of the Negro race and the legitimacy of providing blacks with religious instruction.[14]

III

As he made his way through the city, the missionary from Liberty County noticed, no doubt, not only her churches and the cosmopolitan background of her ministers, but also the black people who swarmed over the streets of Charleston and who were the objects of his missionary concern. Charleston would register at the next census a larger number of black slaves than any other city in the country. Out of a population of almost forty-three thousand, over nineteen thousand were slaves. There were, however, significant differences between these urban slaves and those whom Jones had labored among so faithfully on the plantations of Liberty County.[15]

For one thing, these black slaves lived in a city where the whites were as numerous as the blacks. In contrast to the black slaves of Liberty County who outnumbered the whites almost three to one, the Charleston slaves lived in the midst of a city where they were constantly associated with whites. Rather than the isolation of Liberty County plantations, Charleston blacks were part of a complex urban setting where they could both observe and participate in the life of whites. Here they would be in daily contact not only with their owners and overseers, but also with shopkeepers and tradesmen, neighbors and strangers.

Of even greater significance than their contact with whites, however, was their association with a sizeable number of free blacks. While Liberty County would register at the next census only sixteen free blacks with a slave population of six thousand, Charleston would register over 3,400 free blacks, with a slave population of 19,000. There was, for example, Francis St. Marks. Jones had passed his neat brick house as he had ridden down Meeting Street (the house was next door to Alston Seabrook, a white planter from John's Island). St. Marks was a barber and worked at the luxurious Charleston House Hotel. He not only owned his own home but would later accumulate considerable real estate and a handful of slaves. Obviously a part of a free black elite in Charleston, St. Marks lived and worked on that precarious ground between freedom and slavery. With him in this twilight region were Richard and Joseph Dereef, wealthy speculators in real estate, slave owners, and leaders in the free black community; Richard Kinloch (he pronounced his name like his white cousins: "Kinlaw"), a successful millwright and head of a large family of free blacks; the Noisette family, descendants of Phillipe Noisette, a refugee from Santo Domingo, and his slave Celestine, owners of a prosperous farm at the end of Rutledge Avenue; and John Jones, the city's best known hotelier and owner of a number of valuable lots on Broad Street. These wealthy families were at the top of the economic and social order of free blacks in Charleston. There were, however, many others. Some, like the Holloway family, supported themselves through harnessmaking and other skilled crafts (most were tailors and carpenters, while the others were painters, bricklayers, butchers, barbers, shoemakers or lumber millers). Some secured employment that carried a degree of prestige or operated a small business: Francis Dent was the sexton at the Second Presbyterian Church and Martha Evans had a small grocery; but most free blacks were "slaves without masters," laborers who toiled at menial tasks throughout the city. To be sure, all these free blacks in Charleston suffered severe restrictions on their freedoms, such as the heavy taxes they paid, where they could work, and the constant subordination they were to exhibit—they were forbidden to carry a cane or smoke a pipe in public unless they wanted to run the risk of twenty lashes. Yet, when compared to their slave sisters and brothers, they had important privileges. They could own property, enter certain trades with the right to their earnings, and have the privacy of a home. Additionally, they could have legal marriages and a certain degree of security in their family life.[16]

These free blacks living in the midst of Charleston's large slave population were a reminder that slavery and black skin were not inevitably linked together. Furthermore, the free blacks provided a source of leadership for the blacks of the city and made white control over their slaves much more difficult than on the plantations of Liberty County. "The superior condition of the free persons of color," declared a memorial of Charleston citizens, "excites discontent among our slaves, who continually have before their eyes, persons of the same color, many of whom they have known in slavery, and with all of whom they associate on terms of equality." Slaves can thus see these blacks "freed from control of masters, working where they please, going whither they please, and spending money how they please." The slave thus becomes dissatisfied and "pants after liberty." This envy, however, did not split the black community. "There is an identity of interest," continued the Charleston citizens, "between the slave and the free person of color while there is none between the latter class and the whites." Free blacks and black slaves "are associated by color, connected by marriage, and by friendship. Many of the free negroes have parents, brothers, sisters and children, who are slaves." The free blacks, the white citizens warned, "would have every inducement" to join any insurrection.[17]

For Jones and the others who were gathering to discuss the religious instruction of slaves, this urban setting with its large number of slaves and significant population of free blacks would

mean substantial differences between the approach of the
Charleston churches to the city's black population and the approach of Jones and the Liberty County Association for the Religious Instruction of Negroes. It would be the churches with their
own traditions and histories, and not an association of planters,
that would take the lead in providing religious instruction to
slaves. This would mean for the blacks of Charleston that there
were strong institutional structures in the city that they could use
for their own ends and for the development of the black church.

There was, however, another element in the life of urban slaves
that Jones could not avoid seeing almost immediately upon his
arrival in the city. The week that Jones arrived at this "Capital of
the South" the newspapers of Charleston were advertising a
number of slaves to be sold. There was Julie, "a likely black girl,
about 16, ladies maid, house servant, and handy at her needle,
an excellent child's nurse, warranted sound and healthy." She
was sold at public auction in front of the Custom House. And
there were others, many others. There was Ellen, "a servant,
about 18 years of age, sound and healthy," and Edward, "about
16 years of age, has served three years at the carpenter's trade,
sound and healthy, also an excellent home servant." And there
were the unnamed ones:

> between 50 and 60 likely South Carolina NEGROES, consisting of
> some very superior cooks and washers; plough boys; three house
> boys; able bodied men, rice field and wood cutters; house girls
> from 13 to 17; one prime fellow, a blacksmith; and one elderly
> woman, about 40 years old, a most complete washer and ironer
> and clear starcher.

What a picture this must have presented to the visitor to the city
—young and old waiting to be sold on a fresh spring morning in
front of one of the oldest and finest buildings in Charleston. That
picture, however, was part of Charleston's life, part of a conflict
between aesthetics and ethics that the heart could not avoid.
During the months immediately preceding Jones' visit, hundreds
of black slaves had been sold in the slave markets of Charleston.
Those fine homes that Jones had seen, those seductive gardens

and prestigious and handsome churches, all were based on an economy that demanded that black people with names like Julie and Ellen and Edward be bought and sold.[18]

IV

When Jones arrived at the Adger home, he found an affluent and well-ordered household that reflected many aspects of Charleston's life. James Adger was a Scotch-Irish Presbyterian from Belfast who had made his fortune in Charleston. He had become a cotton broker early and had accumulated enormous wealth as the Cotton Kingdom developed. Expanding into the hardware business, Adger had his own lines of steamers to New York and important connections in European ports. He represented the shipping and commercial interest of Charleston and had little sympathy with the fire-eating parochialism of the planters from the islands and black belt counties around Charleston. An outspoken opponent of nullification, Adger was elected to the state legislature in 1830 as a Unionist and had been a leader among South Carolina Whigs in supporting Henry Clay in 1844. His family spent their summers at the Virginia Springs, at Newport and Saratoga. They went shopping in New York and Philadelphia, visited friends in New Jersey and Boston, and made extended trips to Britain and the continent. One son, John Adger, was a missionary in Armenia where he had translated Jones' catechism for the use of recent converts.[19]

The Adger home was a large, three-story house on the corner of Spring and King Streets. To the right of the Adgers' facing Spring Street was the home of Adger's son-in-law, Thomas Smyth. It, too, was a three-storied house with the third floor given over to Smyth's great library, now numbering almost 15,000 volumes. To the left, facing King Street, was the home of James Adger's son Robert. All three houses were connected through the back yards behind which stood the slave quarters for each home. Across King Street there was a garden with a summer house where the Adger grandchildren played and had their parties. There were beds for vegetables and accomodations for several cows, all of which were under the supervision of the slave "Daddy Daniel."[20]

At the time of Jones' visit, there were at least twenty slaves who lived in the slave quarters behind these three homes. In contrast to the rows of slave cabins some distance from the plantation homes of Liberty County, these slave quarters were intimately connected with the main residences which were located near the street. As was the custom in Charleston, a large brick wall ran around the yards and the quarters, making their residential complex into a kind of compound producing both privacy and confinement. This housing arrangement, added to the large number of blacks and whites associated together in the urban setting, meant that there was unavoidably a familiarity between the races in Charleston that was unknown on the plantations of Liberty County. On the plantations, space was available to keep the slave at a distance; here in Charleston it was impossible to avoid close physical proximity.[21]

John Adger, on his return from his missionary work among the Armenians, would reflect on the nature of this proximity in making a plea for the religious instruction of Charleston blacks. The black slaves "belong to us" said Adger, yet we "also belong to them. They are divided out among us and mingled up with us, and we with them in a thousand ways. They live with us, eating from the same store-houses, drinking from the same fountains, dwelling in the same enclosures, forming parts of the same families."[22]

The Adger complex with this close proximity between blacks and whites was representative of the general housing arrangements for the slaves of Charleston. Most were domestic "servants." A local census in 1848 would reveal that 70% of the adult slaves were listed as "house servants" and these were widely distributed throughout the white families of the city. In the Adger and Smyth households there was, in addition to "Daddy Daniel,"

Peter who was James Adger's coachman; Betsy who was a "house-servant" for Mrs. James Adger, and the wife of Francis Dent, a free man, part Indian, who was the sexton of the Second Presbyterian Church; Betsy and Francis' children Diana, young Betsy, and Sam and John who were Margaret Smyth's "house-servants"; Mom Sue, the Smyth children's nurse, who was "perfectly black and always wore a head-handkerchief" and was married to Joe Corker, a free man, a contractor, who later went to Liberia, taking Mom Sue with him; Caroline and her two children, Amos and Joe; William and his son Harry; Rachel, who did the washing; Caesar, who was "much loved by the Adger grandchildren" and admired because he had fallen out of the second story window and broken a paving stone without material injury to himself; and Jim, who "belonged to Mr. C—" but stayed at the Smyth home because he "was next to starved" by his master. In addition to these, there were the "servants" of Robert Adger's family which no doubt numbered at least five or six.[23]

"The negroes are all well," wrote Margaret Smyth to her sister Susan Adger as she reflected a white mistress' perspective on life within the "family compound." "Mom Sue is quite well—she only lay up one day—but talks a great deal about you and mother.— Betsy is doing quite well now—Caroline makes patato-pone and lives in the bathing house—much to father's distress, who says she burns more firewood than she pays wages—she protests she *buys* her own wood. They are great plagues—your maid Diana has quite a fancy to run into the street at night after she puts the children to bed and I have had some trouble with her.—She is getting to be very impudent.—Lizzie cannot get on with her at all. —I have not employment for them. Rachel has had nothing but the washing of 2 people; but to put them out as Caroline is—is worst—for I have all the noise and bother of her children; and have her sitting about the yard all the time doing nothing.— These negroes are my 'thorn in the flesh'—I do heartily pray to be rid of them.—I must make another complaint to mother.— Somebody last night stole two turkey gobblers wh. she left—and wh. I was keeping for Christmas and New Year. They were very

large and fat and would bring $5 or $6. I have had Richard all
morning looking for them, have sent him down to Market and will
send him again this morning."[24]

The daily life of the Charleston slave, as has been seen from
this glimpse into the Adger and Smyth homes, was quite different
from that of the plantation slave in Liberty County. Caroline, who
was selling potato-pone at the bathing house on the Battery, was
one of many Charleston slaves whose owners found it more
profitable or convenient for them to earn wages rather than work
as domestic servants. Such an arrangement permitted not only
slave vendors such as Caroline, but also slave hirelings engaged
in a wide variety of tasks. While this system provided some economic flexibility to urban slavery, it also permitted a greater
degree of freedom for the slave and loosened the control of the
master over the slave as James Adger's complaint about the firewood intimates.[25]

Diana's "fancy to run into the streets at night" also hints at
another way Charleston slaves sought to claim some freedom for
themselves in the midst of their bondage. Her nighttime trips
might have taken Diana to a number of places. (Jones would have
called them, no doubt, part of "the contaminating influence of
any large town or city.") She could have gone to another "yard"
and visited among the slave quarters of another white family. Or
she could have gone to one of the black shanties that had sprung
up in Charleston Neck and were such a source of anxiety to the
city authorities. Or she could have gone to one of the grog shops
in the Neck. A few months after Jones' visit, the *Charleston Courier*
would be complaining that the Neck was especially "infested with
the lowest and vilest grog shops, poisoning and destroying our
colored population." What Thomas Smyth called "that horrid,
horrid liquor!" had been a problem with some of the Smyth
slaves at an earlier date.[26]

There were, of course, risks, very real dangers, for Diana or any
other Charleston black to act in an "impudent" manner or to seek
some nighttime claim of personal freedom. If they went beyond
the patience of their owners or were discovered abroad at night,

they could be whipped and whipped severely. In Liberty County an owner or overseer would have to whip raw and bleeding backs, see and hear the pain, and be an active participant in the cruelty. It was an ugly enough scene to make sensitive owners reluctant to use the whip (although the isolation of the plantation also gave opportunity for greater cruelty). In Charleston, however, there was the efficiency and impersonality possible in an urban setting. Owners could send their slaves to the workhouse to be whipped out-of-sight and out-of-hearing, and, to heighten the degradation, the slaves would have to carry the instructions for their whipping along with the twenty-five cents to cover the charges. If a Charleston white still did not want a slave to return to the "family compound" with a bleeding back, there was the treadmill which, it was said, caused even greater fear among the Charleston blacks: six would tread at the same time on each wheel, while six rested on a bench behind the wheel; the left hand person would step off every half minute, the other five would move one place to the left, and the right hand person on the bench would move onto the empty position at the wheel. Working three minutes, resting three minutes, the slaves would tread eight hours a day.[27]

The workhouse, however, was not the only means whites had of attempting to discipline the slave community in Charleston: there were the churches. Both the church's teaching and discipline would be applied to keep the slaves "in their place," more submissive to the white masters and mistresses, and also free from any illicit activities that a nighttime excursion might involve.

Ironically enough, however, the churches of Charleston had already become centers for black activities and provided the slaves of the city with opportunities for freedoms not known in other areas of their lives. Here the leaders of the black community were nurtured. Here blacks had organized so that even in the midst of their bondage they could support one another's spiritual and physical needs. Here, in the churches of the city, black slaves had laid the foundation for the black church which in the years ahead would seek to lead their people out of Egypt into the Promised Land.

6

"If These Be Brothers..."

I

When Jones arrived at the meeting on Chalmers Street, he could see the cultural and political leaders of the city gathering to discuss the religious instruction of black slaves. There was Daniel Huger who would be presiding over the meeting. Of distinguished Huguenot descent (Charlestonians liked to surprise visitors with the pronunciation of his name—*you-gee*), he had long been involved in South Carolina politics and was now serving in the United States Senate. Huger was a Unionist and had opposed Calhoun and others over the nullification controversy during the 1830's. With him was Joel Poinsett who as a Congressman had joined with Huger and other Unionists against Calhoun and his forces. Educated in England, Poinsett had had a distinguished diplomatic career, had traveled through Russia and South America and had brought back from Mexico the flower which would bear his name—the poinsettia.[1]

Jones could see, however, that Unionists were by no means the only political leaders who came to the meeting. There was Robert

Barnwell Rhett, the "fire-eater" from James Island who would be elected to the Senate after Calhoun's death and who would earn the dubious distinction of being "father of the Secession." The piety that now brought Rhett to this meeting on the religious instruction of slaves would later lead him, as he came to sign the Ordinance of Secession, to kneel and pray silently over it. With Rhett was C. G. Memminger, a young lawyer, who would one day serve as Secretary of the Treasury for the Confederate States of America, and Robert Barnwell, President of the South Carolina College and future Confederate Senator.[2]

In addition to these political figures, Jones saw what looked like a gathering of Charleston's exclusive St. Cecilia Society. There was Charles Cotesworth Pinckney, Daniel Ravenel, Charles Lowndes, Thomas Pinckney Alston, Thomas Drayton Grimké, and Grimké Drayton—all wealthy planters whose families had long been prominent in the state and had provided leading patriots during the Revolution. From among this aristocratic group, Jones no doubt found Thomas Drayton Grimké of particular interest. What would Sara and Angelina Grimké, those two fiery abolitionist sisters now living in the North, think of their older and best-loved brother attending a meeting on the religious instruction of slaves?[3]

Jones joined a number of other ministers gathering for the meeting. The Episcopal Church was represented by Stephen Elliott, Bishop of Georgia, and William Barnwell, pastor of St. Peters in Charleston. William Capers, the Methodist minister, was here. Only the week before he had returned to Charleston from Louisville, Kentucky, where he had been a vigorous participant in the organizing convention of the Methodist Episcopal Church, South, which had recently split with northern Methodists over the question of slavery. Now after helping to organize a southern Methodist church that would be vigorous in its defense of the South's "peculiar institution," Capers was back in Charleston to provide much firsthand information on the religious instruction of slaves. Richard Fuller, a Baptist minister from Beaufort, had also just arrived in Charleston—he straight from the first meeting of the Southern Baptist Convention. Like the Methodists, the Baptists had divided over the question of slavery and Fuller himself had recently completed a long scholarly argument over the nature of slavery with President Francis Wayland of Brown College—the country's best-known moral philosopher. In addition to these men, Jones could see that Thomas Smyth and John Bachman were both here, as was Jones' old friend Benjamin Gildersleeve who was editor of the *Charleston Observer,* a weekly religious newspaper with a wide distribution in the lower South. Gildersleeve's father had been for nineteen years the pastor of the Midway Church and had baptized Jones in 1804. But Gildersleeve and Jones were not the only ones here from Liberty County. There was old Dr. William McWhir who had taught Jones as a boy and had married Charles and Mary Jones in 1830. He had come to Charleston with Thomas Clay, a wealthy planter and longtime friend of the Jones family.[4]

II

Gathering in the Depository of Chalmers Street, this distinguished group of southern whites began their deliberations on the religious instructions of the black slaves of the South. Questionnaires had been sent out earlier requesting information from interested persons and the replies were now read. Robert Barnwell Rhett, Daniel Ravenel, Robert Barnwell, and Daniel Huger began an animated discussion. What was the best means of providing religious instruction? Can black teachers or preachers be used safely? Should blacks and whites worship together? What is the influence of the master's personal interest and his example? What influence does religious instruction have on the labor, discipline, and good order of the slaves?[5]

For three days the discussions went on. Thomas Grimké gave a report on his personal practices as a master (he was kind, but he could never convince his sisters Sara and Angelina that slavery was a benevolent system). Robert Barnwell Rhett told how he developed the piety and good order among his James Island slaves, and Jones and Richard Fuller delivered addresses on "the religious instruction of the negroes."[6]

The primary difficulty which these white Southerners faced was exemplified by the very location of their meeting place. They had gathered on Chalmers Street to discuss how to convert and nurture black people in the Christian faith. Yet on that very street and on the streets around them black men and women, boys and girls, were being bought and sold. On the same day that this distinguished group of whites gathered, a "likely" group of blacks were being gathered together to be sold only a few doors down Chalmers Street at Thomas Ryan's slave market. The distinction of these blacks was marked in their advertisement:

A family of 5 field Negroes, consisting of 2 able Women, 2 likely girls, 10 and 14 years old, and a likely Boy, 12 years old.

A family of 3 field Negroes, 2 Women and a Boy 15 years old.

2 Women, field hands, mother and daughter, very likely.

4 prime Fellows, field hands and good axemen.

1 prime Fellow, first rate plowman and wagoner.

A Boy 15 years old, has served 3 years at the Taylor's trade.

A young Woman, seamstress and ladies' maid, with her son, 6 years old.

A colored Girl, 17 years old.

2 single Girls, 9 and 12 years old.

A Woman, good cook, washer and ironer, with her son, a likely colored Boy, 13 years old, a good house servant.

An elderly Woman, good cook, washer and ironer.

A single Boy, 10 years old.

And two Women field hands.[7]

How would white Southerners tell these black people about God's love and justice, mercy and judgment? How would a slave master or mistress call the families of these slaves to be their Christian brothers or sisters? At the conclusion of the meeting a committee was given the task to reflect on the discussions and to write "An Address to the Public." They were to attempt to give some justification for whites' providing religious instruction to these black slaves.[8]

III

The providence of God, they declared, has been at work in the mystery of these human affairs. How could black slaves be in the Promised Land of America except through the providence of God? For, through that providence, whites have had placed in their hands both these dependent black slaves and "divine revelation." It is, therefore, the *duty* of whites to impart this revelation to their black slaves. It whites fail in their responsibility to those who are so dependent upon them, they can expect nothing but God's displeasure. If, however, whites were to accept their responsibility, it would mean the religious character of both the master and the slave would be improved. For the slave it would mean receiving the blessings of the gospel and its moral influences. For the master it would mean a good influence upon his own character. For, the Charlestonians declared, we "can scarcely impart, without also receiving the influences of Christian light and action."[9]

The responsibility of whites for the religious instruction of these black slaves was thus a duty which whites could not avoid. The providence of God had laid upon southern whites an important task in the contemporary evangelical campaign to convert America and make it a truly Christian nation. To evangelize and nurture the black slave in the Christian faith was one part, a particularly southern part, of the total mission of American Christians.

Alongside of this evangelical concern, however, the Address made it clear, just as Jones had done in Liberty County, that the religious instruction of blacks was believed to have "a salutary effect" upon their labor and discipline. (It was, after all, an area of great interest to these pious slaveholders, though dangerous to be too open about it!) The reports received in reply to the circulars sent out had given "a gratifying testimony" about the "effect of the religious instruction of Negroes, upon *laborer,* and upon discipline." "It would indeed be strange," it was declared, if religious instruction based on the love of God and love to our neighbor "worked no restraints, furnished no direction and inspired no desires or hopes connected with well-doing." At the same time, such religious instruction would also have its effects on the manner in which the white owners undertook their responsibilities. It would lead to a wise management and to a discipline "mild, regular, and beneficial to master and slave." The results were thus clear: good and obedient slaves, kind and pious masters.[10]

The motivation for bringing religious instruction to black slaves was, therefore, neither purely religious nor purely economic. On the contrary, religious and social forces were closely interwoven. There was a reciprocal relationship between the two. "We cannot separate," the Address insisted, "in any just view of the economy of life, its spiritual and temporal interests: and we delude ourselves, when we suppose, that any worldly purposes are permanently advanced upon purely worldly principles. A wise management would combine kindness with discipline and aim at making labor effective, and the laborer happy. But these ends can only be effected by moral causes; causes that act upon character —that form or reform the moral being."[11]

If religious influences played an important part in shaping the manner in which an owner would treat a slave and the way in which a slave would go about his or her tasks, social influences also played an important part in shaping the religious instruction. This was especially true as those social influences were expressed in "public opinion." These Charlestonians and their friends were only too well aware that in the slave holding states "there is a public opinion, a common law of sentiment, which influences and controls . . . the general management of our Negro population." You had to be careful, very careful, with the South's peculiar institution. Public opinion was thus an important influence both on the method used for the religious instruction and on the content of that instruction. Yet even here, they would continue to insist that there was a reciprocal relationship between religious and social forces. For the religious influence, it was hoped, would "elevate and improve that public opinion, with which the true interests of the relation of master and slave, both spiritual and temporal, are so closely associated."[12]

The nature of the interaction between these religious and social factors meant that all attempts to bring religious instruction to the black slave would be decidedly paternalistic in character.[13] They would be paternalistic because they would be eminently personal and would at the same time emphasize the ideal of stability and order in society. The white owners with their "sense of duty" toward both the black slave and southern society would be in complete control. The point of emphasis would be the *personal* relationship between the owner and slave, rather than the social structures of society, while the society itself would be viewed as an organic whole with each person having a place in the total order.

This paternalism was the primary way in which these Charlestonians justified their attempts to convert and nurture in the Christian faith the black slave. It was based upon an apparent duality in the New Testament. Quoting St. Peter, they declared that "God is no respector of persons." As St. Paul insisted in his Letter to the Ephesians, "God is the master of masters as well as slaves." Yet St. Paul had also declared, "Slaves, be obedient to those who are your earthly masters, with fear and trembling in singleness of heart as to Christ." In light of eternity, the distinctions between masters and slaves were of little significance. The gospel message was for all classes of people. It was designed, said the Address, for all humanity, and although "in the doubtless wise providence of God, all classes do not seem, to human judgment, equally favored in their opportunities, we know that *all* are objects of his care. . . ." Yet it was precisely because all people were brothers and sisters in Christ that temporal distinctions were of little importance. The terms "brother" or "sister" could be used by white masters and mistresses in speaking of their black slaves because these words carried for them the meaning of a mutual relationship to God and had no reference to a person's place in society or to any type of social equality.[14]

This distinguished group of southern whites thus concluded and published to the world that all people are brothers and sisters—spiritual brothers and sisters in Christ. Of course, they insisted, there are divisions in this world, there are differences between those who gather to debate and discuss and those who are gathered at Thomas Ryan's to be auctioned and sold. But in the blinding light of what Christ has done for humanity's eternal salvation, what are the distinctions between these two gatherings on Chalmers Street? Were they not all saved by grace? Were they not all children of the same God?

Here then was the call and the justification for the religious instruction of black slaves. It gave significant community support and theoretical undergirding for the work that Jones had been building in Liberty County. The paternalistic framework of the task would mean that concerned whites could both accept the existing social structures and seek to work within them. They would not try to abolish the system of slavery, but they could try to make it more humane. They could try to follow a middle way; they could try to treat their black slaves as spiritual brothers and sisters without seeking to free them from their cruel bondage.

IV

In the fall of 1845, only a few months after the meeting on the religious instruction of slaves, Louis Agassiz, the brilliant Swiss naturalist and professor at Harvard, addressed the Charleston Literary and Philosophic Society and offered a profound challenge to those whites who sought to provide religious instruction to the black slave. He spoke on the plural origin of the races: because the black and white races were so diverse, said Agassiz, and because in nature one type always remains the same, there must have been a different origin for each race. It was a simple enough proposition by a respected scientist, but it was filled with dangerous implications about the humanity of the Negro and the possibility of providing religious instruction to the black race.[15]

Agassiz's position on the dual origin of the races offered to an anxious South the perfect defense of its peculiar institution: an ethnological justification of slavery. Its fundamental principle, which went back as far as the speculations of Aristotle, was that slavery grew out of an inequality of nature. Through the application of new information derived from the natural sciences and through the use of anatomy and anthropology, some Southerners had begun to gather and to analyze carefully a large array of facts on which to build a positive philosophy of slavery. From the result of their labor they were to maintain that slavery did not arise from any disorder in nature or from the struggle for racial supremacy, but developed out of nature's well ordered plan.[16]

The problem for these scientific defenders of slavery was how to verify and substantiate the inferiority of the Negro. It was a question of demonstrating that the faculties of the Negro, as compared to those of the white person, qualified Negroes only for a state of slavery and made them unfit for freedom or, incidentally, for the benefits of the gospel. It was only necessary to prove that the Negro race was weak and poorly developed in mind and body, and hence a member of a lower order, in order to justify slavery and make futile any attempts at the religious instruction of the slave.

History and physiology were used in an effort to prove the natural inferiority of the Negro. Drawing from a comparative study of the races throughout the course of history, it was concluded by some whites that the Negro had always occupied a servile position. Egyptian painting and sculpture showed that the Negro had been the slave of the Egyptian. Those times that the Negro had gained freedom, it was claimed that barbarism was one result, with Santo Domingo as the most vivid illustration. Even the free blacks of the United States, it was claimed, were considered by whites "the most worthless and indolent" of the nation's citizens.[17]

In addition to the "facts of history" there was the composition of the Negro's body. Comparative anatomy was used to point out the peculiarities of the black person and to note the many differences from the white race in the organization of the brain, the nerves, and the vital organs. Agassiz described what he saw as the differences between the brain of the Negro and the Caucasian:

> A peculiar conformation characterized the brain of the adult negro. Its development never gets beyond that observable in the Caucasian in boyhood. And besides other singularities, it bears a striking resemblance, in several particulars, to the brain of an ourang-outang.[18]

All of these differences, so the argument went, indicated the reason for the black's status as a slave. Blacks were held to be imitative, never creative; they were lazy and indolent, opposed to exertion and unable to create a civilization of their own. Because of all these characteristics, the black was perfectly fit for a state of slavery. But more than this, it was claimed that these differences between the races indicated that the Negro was a separate species from the white race.

Agassiz's address before the Charleston Literary and Philosophic Society brought all of the arguments to the fore with his claim of a dual origin of the races. Blacks and whites, he declared, do not spring from the same source but flow from separate fountain heads. The diversity of the races and the permanency of racial types indicate that blacks and whites are separate species and are derived from different origins. How then could they be brothers and sisters—even spiritual brothers and sisters—to those who belonged to the superior white race? Dr. John Barrett, a transplanted Englishman, enthusiastically saw the implications of Agassiz's position and serenaded the Medical Association of South Carolina with these grotesque lines:

> And I said, if these are brothers how changed
> From white to black, and from lank to curly hair
> With flattened nose, retreating forehead,
> Short chin, and uncouth thickened lips,
> As if fancy and nature had combined
> To mar the godlike form and face of man.[19]

V

John Bachman and Thomas Smyth sat listening to Agassiz's address and immediately realized the profound ethical and theological implications of his theory of a dual origin of the races. Both clergymen were repulsed; they protested vigorously and at once set about refuting Agassiz's claims and upholding the unity of the races. For the next three years the major part of their scholarly efforts would be turned in this direction, and they would produce the two most outstanding books of the period upholding the unity of the races.[20]

John Bachman, as an eminent naturalist, relied primarily upon analogies from the animal kingdom and upon his careful study of the nature of a species. For Bachman humanity was clearly a single species in the animal kingdom. This could be seen through the laws of hybridity:

> Since no two species of animals have ever been known to produce a prolific hybrid race, therefore hybridity is a test of specific character.
> Consequently the fact that all the races of mankind produce with each other a fertile progeny, by which means new varieties have been produced in every country, constitutes one of the most pow-

erful and undeniable arguments in favour of the unity of the races.[21]

In other words, horses and donkeys are different species because their hybrid offspring, the mule, is incapable of reproducing. The mulatto, however, does reproduce, thus proving the parent races are of the same species since the definition of a species was based on the ability to produce fertile offspring.

While Smyth would spend three years studying at the medical college in preparation for his book, *Unity of the Human Races,* he did not rely on scientific research as heavily as Bachman. Smyth turned primarily to the history of black civilization and culture and to the testimony of the Bible. In three chapters on the "Former Civilization of Black Races of Men," Smyth presented a wide range of historical and anthropological evidence showing that "dark or black races, with more or less of the negro physiognomy, were in the earliest period of their known history cultivated and intelligent, having kingdoms, arts, and manufacturers." There was no indication, declared Smyth, that Negro slavery was not of modern origin. "The degradation of this race of men therefore, must be regarded as the result of external causes, and not of natural, inherent and original incapacity."[22]

Bachman and Smyth, both of whom had already given years of labor for the religious instruction of blacks, were horrified by the theological and ethical implications of any theory that denied the essential unity of the races. The gospel, declared Smyth,

> must stand or fall with the doctrine of the unity of the human races. For if, as it is alleged, the Caucasian race ALONE have any interest in the revelations, the promises, and the threatenings of the Bible, then it follows that the gospel ought not to be preached to any other than TRUE AND GENUINE CAUCASIAN MEN. But where and how are these to be found? Amid the incalculable intermixture of races which has taken place among men since the beginning of time, where is the man who can prove he is a pure Caucasian? There is NOT ONE. And, therefore, there is not one who can dare to preach or to hear the gospel.[23]

While Bachman and Smyth would both be accused of being abolitionists for supporting the unity of the races, they did not hesitate to call into question the motives of those who insisted that the black was a different species and therefore of a lower order than the white race. A primary motivation for such a theory, declared Smyth, was to "degrade the African below the standard of human species in order to justify his barbarous and unjust treatment. . . ." The theory had been adopted and widely diffused among Southerners "upon the very ground of its apparent justification of inhumanity to man."[24]

Let the South beware, warned Smyth. The practical effects of such a degrading theory would be "inexpedient and suicidal to the South in the maintenance of her true relations to her coloured population." The black would not be recognized as a fellow-being and the South would become a scene of conflict between white and black, between "avarice and cunning, power and hatred, cruelty and revenge." If the South adopted this theory as her ultimate defense of slavery and denied the humanity of the black person, the only basis for the reconciliation of Christianity with slavery would be overthrown. Divine providence, Smyth insisted, had brought blacks to the South in order that eternal salvation might come to them. God would bring good out of evil, light out of darkness, and would cause the institution of slavery to work for the equal good of both masters and servants. White Southerners, declared both Smyth and Bachman, must emphatically reject any racial theory that would deny the humanity of the black, and must exercise the high and responsible duties of masters to those to whom divine providence had placed in their care.[25]

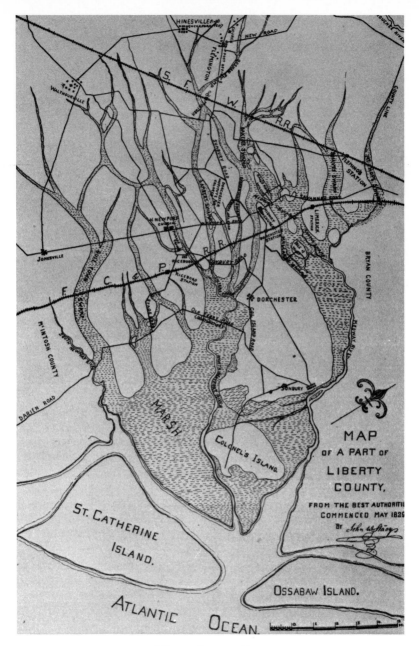

Liberty County Map

Charleston, 1850

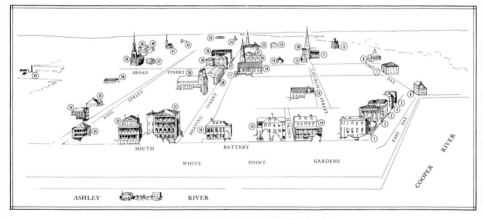

BIRD'S-EYE VIEW OF CHARLESTON 1850

1. De Saussure House
2. Roper House
3. William Ravenel House
4. Holmes House (Gone)
5. Edmonston-Alston House
6. Capt. Missroon House
7. Vander Horst Row
8. The Exchange
9. Proposed Custom House
10. St. Philip's Church
11. The Huguenot Church

12. Charleston Library Society
13. The First Baptist Church
14. Capt. Welsman House
15. William Washington House
16. Gourdin House
17. South Carolina Society
18. St. Michael's Church
19. Daniel Ravenel House
20. City Hall
21. Fireproof Building
    Home now of the S. C.
    Historical Society

22. The Circular Church
23. Cumberland Methodist
24. Second Presbyterian Church
25. The Old Citadel
26. The Hibernian Hall
27. The Court House
28. The Hebrew Orphan Society
29. The Guard House
30. Scotch Presbyterian Church
31. Ross House
32. Stevens House

33. Ashe House
34. Lamboll House
35. Miles Brewton House
36. St. Peter's Church
37. St. Andrew's Hall
38. St. Finbar's Cathedral
39. The Unitarian Church
40. St. John's Lutheran Church
41. Grace Church
42. St. Paul's, Radcliffeborough
43. Chisolm's Rice Mill

Second Presbyterian Church

Zion Church

Charles C. Jones

William Capers

Margaret Adger Smyth

Cordially yours
John B. Adger

John B. Adger

Richard Allen

Morris Brown

Daniel Payne

"Old Quarterman," Born in Slavery

LIST OF NEGROES---CONTINUED.

	No.	NAMES.	Age.	QUALIFICATIONS.
1000	36	Beck,	26	Prime field hand.
200	37	Young Tanah,	3	
50	3 38	Infant.		*570*
0-0	39	Marilla,	70	Old, gardener,
650	40	Fanny,	38	Prime field hand.
1200	41	Phillip,	18	Field hand,
1000	42	Sylvia,	16	" "
950	5—43	Emanuel,	14	*725*
500	1—44	Frank,	50	Coachman. *550*
0-0	45	Old Linda,	70	Nurse,
500	46	Dinah,	42	Field hand.
1150	47	Ansel,	18	" "
1000	48	Becca,	16	" " Mrs. B.
2100	49	Annie,	5	
200	6—50	Ellen,	3	*570* Mrs. B.
400	51	Catherine,	50	Field Hand,
1250	52	John,	28	" "
1000	53	Young Linda,	26	" " Mrs. B.
1200	4—54	Joshua,	24	" " *930*
900	55	Sylvia,	30	Plain Cook and washer.
850	56	Joe,	12	Prime boy.
750	57	Jim,	10	" "
400	58	Isaiah,	5	Lost one eye,
200	59	Cimon,	3	Mrs. B.
00	6—60	Mariah		Infant. *490*
700	61	Margaret,	40	House servant and cook.
1100	62	Susan,	20	Half witted.
850	63	Adam,	12	Prime boy Mrs. B.
1100	74	Lavinia,	18	Chamber maid.
50	5—65	Rose,		Infant. *475* Mrs. B.
1100	66	Nanny,	25	Seamstress and chambermaid.
1100	2—67	Infant.	1	*755* Mrs. B.

Total $ 27160

average $ 3270

A Charleston Slave Sale

COMMUNICANTS' ROLL BOOK.

NAME.	Servant of PLACE OF RESIDENCE.	Employment or Profession.	DATE OF ADMISSION Year.	Month.
Henry Frazer	Mr. J. A. Cook		1857	Sept.
John Warren	Mr. Elisha Whilden		"	"
James Brown	Mr. Allen Boyle		"	"
Sarah Brown	Mr. James Ross		"	"
Rosina Morris	Free		"	"
Emma Mackey	Free		"	"
Henry Green	Miss Matthews		"	"
Richard Lowndes	Mrs. Wilson		"	"
Flora Brown	Miss Tunno		"	"
Minda Thomson	Mrs. Tunno		"	"
[James Holmes]	Mr. Clarence Murray		"	"
Venus Girardeau	Rev. John L. Girardeau		"	"
Caroline Small	Mr. J. Small		"	"
Elsy Elsworth				
Susan Elsworth				

Communicants' Roll Book, Zion Church

Liberty County Grave Markers

Charleston Slave Quarters

Charleston "Servant Houses" Behind White Residence

Charleston Harness Shop Owned by Free Blacks

Anson Street Chapel

Calvary Episcopal Church

Midway Congregational Church

St. Michael's Episcopal Church

Old Bethel Methodist Church

First Baptist Church

Interior, First (Scots) Presbyterian Church

Angelina Grimké

Francis L. Cardozo

John L. Girardeau

John Bachman

Charles and Lucy at the Grave of Charles Jones

7

A Slave's Sabbath

I

Early on a Sunday morning in 1845, black people of Charleston, dressed in their best clothes, began to make their way toward the proud old churches of the city. Emerging from the cramped and enclosed slave quarters behind elegant Charleston homes and from the shanties on Charleston Neck, they walked the sand and cobblestone streets as the sky began to pale in the east beyond the Battery. It was a slave's Sabbath in this "Capital of the South" —a day that would present startling contrasts as it revealed both the ironic pretensions of paternalistic whites and the enduring courage and faith of a people held in bondage.

Almost half the blacks of Charleston were on their way to church. They went as a people who carried not only the hopes and fears of the human heart but the pain and weight of slavery. Yet they also went as a people who knew where they were going, for they were familiar with the Charleston churches. Just as they were "divided out among and mingled up with" the white families of the city, so were they divided out and mingled up among the churches of Charleston. The difference was that, while they could not choose their white "family," they had some choice as to their church.

The largest group of blacks made their way to Trinity Methodist Church on the corner of Hazel Street and Maiden Lane. So many would gather here to worship that unruly whites called it "a nigger church." In fact, blacks flocked to all three Methodist churches in the city, outnumbering the whites almost seven to one. During the next fifteen years the Methodist churches would average a total white membership of only five to seven hundred while the black membership would average between four and five thousand. A typical year would find the following breakdown[1]:

	Whites	
	In Full Connection	*On Probation*
Trinity Methodist	293	10
Cumberland Methodist	179	10
Bethel Methodist	164	35
	Blacks	
	In Full Connection	*On Probation*
Trinity Methodist	1806	450
Cumberland Methodist	1157	253
Bethel Methodist	1152	262

The white Methodists of Charleston, complained the Methodist minister F. A. Mood, have to live with the jealous taunt that "Methodism is successful among the negroes, because it is only suited to them." "My heart sinketh," Bishop Asbury had written of the early Methodist labors in Charleston, "and I am ready to conclude we are not sent to the whites in this place, except a very few; but to the poor Africans." The few hundred whites who did attend a Methodist church on Sunday morning were often troubled if not overwhelmed by the blacks who crowded the balconies and overflowed the sanctuaries. In earlier years they had been harassed and their preachers subjected to the assaults of disorderly mobs. Even the venerable Bishop Asbury had been insulted by a mob that had greeted his arrival at church with "sneers, hurrahs, and shouts." "I lament the wickedness of this city," wrote Asbury, "and their great hatred against us." Had Methodism of Charleston, reflected Mood in later years, "courted the favor of the wealthy, and kissed the feet of political aspirants, and let go her hold and interest upon the blacks, she too might have claimed the favor of those who affected to despise her; but her mission was to spread holiness and save souls," and she would not turn from her task because of her opposition and the contempt of her enemies. Gradually, however, the white Methodists of the city had shown themselves to be friends of slavery, so that, by the time blacks came pouring into sanctuaries on a Sunday morning in 1845, the Methodist churches had become part of the city's establishment.[2]

While the largest number of blacks would go to one of the Methodist churches, many also headed to one of the Baptist churches of Charleston—especially the First Baptist. Walking down narrow Church Street past rows of town houses, they found in a stately old sanctuary of classical design a large and vigorous congregation of blacks and whites who worshipped together the carpenter of Galilee. In many ways their situation was similar to that of the Methodist churches, for the blacks heavily outnumbered the whites not only here but in the two other Baptist churches in the city as well[3]:

	Whites	Blacks
First Baptist	293	1543
Wentworth Street	178	392
Morris Street	33	56

In spite of these figures, the white Baptists never seem to have been troubled by the jeers which the Methodists received. Several prominent white families attended the First Baptist Church, and the church itself was one of the oldest in the city.

In addition to the Methodist and Baptist churches, blacks also headed on a sabbath morning toward St. Michael's and St. Philip's Episcopal Churches, to the Circular Congregational Church, First (Scots) Presbyterian, Second Presbyterian, and St. John's Lutheran Church. Here, however, their numbers were generally only half that of the white membership. The Second Presbyterian Church, for example, had 380 white members in 1845 and 178 black members, while St. John's Lutheran Church had 398 whites and 198 blacks.[4]

Those blacks who gathered for mass at one of Charleston's Roman Catholic churches were primarily slaves, or their desendants, who had come with Roman Catholic owners from Santo Domingo. Most of these attended St. Mary's where French had long been—with Latin—the language of worship. The other black Roman Catholics would go to St. Finbar's Cathedral. (St. Paul's Church was made up of predominantly German laborers and small shopkeepers with no black members.) At the Cathedral, Bishop England had attempted in the 1830's to organize a public school for black children which he had been forced to close when legislation had been passed closing all the black schools in the city. The Bishop was a native of Ireland whose extraordinary energy had made him a leader of the American Catholic hierarchy. England, however, because of the anti-Catholicism of the period, was greatly concerned that Catholics as a group should not be set apart unnecessarily from other citizens. His *Letters* to John Forsyth, United States Secretary of State, presented the Roman Catholic position on slavery and came to be regarded as an authoritative expression of Catholic opinion. These *Letters* were received in Charleston as a vindication of southern slavery and reflected the Roman Church's turning away from its earlier attempts to reach the blacks of the city.[5]

As black slaves made their way toward these different Charleston churches, they apparently headed for the church of their own choosing. Except for those who were Roman Catholics, they often did not attend the same churches as their masters or mistresses. Indeed, just the opposite often seems to have been the case, for church rolls reveal that blacks, both free and slave, moved with ease between the different churches in the city and changed their membership as frequently as did the whites. What they apparently did was to go to those churches that took their needs most seriously and provided them with the most freedom and the best opportunities for black leadership.[6]

One thing, however, was certain—the churches were controlled by whites no matter how many blacks might attend. The church property was owned by whites, the government and discipline of the churches was directed by whites, the preaching was generally white oriented and the ministers devoted most of their time to the whites in the congregations. All of this, no doubt, made it difficult for the blacks in Charleston, as well as in Liberty County, to have a deep sense of belonging to one particular congregation. Slaves, after all, belonged to masters and mistresses and not to congregations, no matter how close their ties. Still, the blacks went to the churches of the city and claimed a belonging that transcended the ownership of whites or even of congregations: they were brothers and sisters, a people who belonged to Jesus, children of God. The tension between this not belonging and yet belonging would clearly mark their sabbath day activities and all their relationships with the churches of Charleston. It would mean they would participate in the life of the congregations as the familiar guests of the white members, yet they would be guests who knew Another to be their host.

II

Arriving at church early on Sunday morning, the black people of Charleston divided into classes with one of their own as leader or watchman. Here in their classes with their own leaders they found the focal point of their church life. They would begin with singing and prayer and have a Scripture reading and an exhortation on Christian duties. For some there would be a catechism lesson. Most would use Jones' catechism with its hymns and prayers, Apostles' Creed and Scripture lessons, as well as its questions and answers about sin and judgment, grace and salvation, masters and servants. (One wonders how often or with what knowing glances these last questions and answers were given.) "I know that your generous heart would be all set on fire," wrote a patronizing white visitor of one of the classes at St. John's Lutheran Church, "if you could once mingle with them, and take part in their simple, but I firmly believe, honest efforts to worship God."[7]

In many ways the class leaders were the black preachers in Charleston. They included in their number both free blacks and slaves. While few of them could openly claim the title "preacher," they did function as pastors to their own people and as leaders in the black community. They had many of the same responsibilities that Sam and Toney and the other black leaders in Liberty County had—only their responsibilities were more extensive for a complex urban setting and reflected the differences between the city and the plantation. There was Thomas Catto, a free black, who was clearly the outstanding leader among the blacks who attended the Second Presbyterian Church and the "first among equals" of the class leaders. (In 1845 there were nine, three of whom were free.) He met with his class weekly and visited the members regularly in their homes. He introduced and recommended to the white minister and session those who wished to become communing members of the church. When a member was found sick or in need, he arranged as their leader for a small stipend from the poor fund. When differences arose between members or when a member's conduct was questionable, he reported to the minister and session for the possible exercise of church discipline. And finally, when a member died, following the religious service by the minister, Catto took charge of committing the body to the grave.[8]

Catto and the other leaders at the Second Presbyterian Church were allowed to "exhort" but not to "preach." They could lead their classes with prayer and singing and could exhort "their brethren briefly and modestly when moved to do so," but they

were "strictly prohibited all such utterances as by their length, or
their formality and pretension may be likely to present them
before the people in the attitude of Ministers of Jesus Christ."
Similar restrictions were evidently placed on the black leaders of
other churches, not only because of the widespread fear in the
South of black preachers—clearly the most important reason—
but also because of the formal educational requirements some of
the churches had for ministers. At the Circular Congregational
Church, the black leaders could not preach on a text, but they
could read the Scriptures, pray, lead singing and exhort. At the
First Baptist Church, however, with its sectarian traditions, blacks
were licensed to preach. Thus a special committee was appointed
in 1850 to hear "Brother Jacob Legare exercise his gifts," and he
was licensed to join Ned Laurens and Thomas Bell as "one of the
colored preachers" of the congregation.[9]

These black leaders were, in surprising numbers, literate. The
laws of the state and ordinances of the city prohibited any black,
slave or free, from being taught to read or write under a penalty
not exceeding $100 fine and six months imprisonment for a white
person and not exceeding $50 fine and fifty lashes for a free
person of color. Yet throughout the churches of Charleston,
black leaders were reading the Scriptures publicly to their classes
and submitting written reports to white church officers. There
were simply too many opportunities in Charleston for blacks to
learn to read for the laws to be completely effective. Unlike the
isolation of Liberty County plantations, Charleston provided
newspapers and street signs, shops and access to books and pamphlets. Moreover, there was in Charleston a tradition of black
leaders who managed even in the midst of a slave system to
obtain the fundamentals of an education and who had succeeded
in transmitting it to others in the black community.[10]

There had been, for example, Daniel Payne, a free black leader
in the Methodist Church. He had attended for two years the
Minors' Moralist Society which had been organized by a group
of free blacks. Its purpose was to "educate orphan or indigent
colored children, and also to provide for their necessary wants."

When he was about ten years old, Payne had entered the school
of "Mr. Thomas Bonneau, the most popular school-master in the
city." Bonneau was a wealthy free black, a member of the elite
Brown Fellowship Society, and a teacher of free blacks in the city
for over twenty years. Payne had studied with him for three.
"There," he wrote

> I learned to spell, read, and write, and "cipher" as far as the "Rule
> of Three." The chief books used for reading were monographs of
> the histories of Greece, Rome, and England; while the "Colum-
> bian Orator" was used for training in the art of speaking.

When Payne was thirteen, he entered the carpenter's trade with
his brother-in-law James Holloway; yet he continued to study,
staying up late at night poring over a variety of subjects from
religion to geography and zoology. Books were hard for a black
in Charleston to come by legitimately, and it was necessary for
him to "find" some and "borrow" others from the white libraries
in the city. By the time he was nineteen, Payne was ready to open
his own school. For six years he taught up to sixty students before
being forced to close by new legislation in 1835. The white ministers John Bachman and Benjamin Palmer had been supporters of
his school (Bachman had been interested in his scientific studies
and shared his own research) and sought both to console him in
its closing and open the way for a new start in the North.[11]

While Payne was in many ways exceptional, he reflected the
ability of a number of black leaders in Charleston, both free and
slave, to gain at least the fundamentals of a formal education.
Indeed, some whites who were concerned about the religious
instruction of blacks even began, against the general public sentiment, to advocate the repeal of laws prohibiting the teaching of
reading and writing. Judge Belton O'Neal, who attended the
meeting on religious instruction in 1845 and who codified the
"Negro Law in South Carolina," reflected that "as Christians
how can we justify it that a slave is not permitted to read the
Bible? It is vain to say there is danger in it. The best slaves in the
state are those who can and do read the scriptures. Do not our

own sons and daughters teach the slaves to read? Such laws look to me as rather cowardly. It seems as if we were afraid of our slaves. Such a feeling is unworthy of a Carolina master." Years later Mary Veal, a former slave of Judge O'Neal, would remember that the judge's daughter had, in fact, taught her to read.[12]

By whatever means they were able to gain the opportunity to learn to read and write, black leaders in the Charleston churches had a wider world opened to them through this precious knowledge. By having direct access to the Bible and by being able to read books and newspapers, they could speak with authority in the black community. They could move through the printed word beyond the white control that sought to isolate the blacks. They could leap beyond Charleston and the South to a free world that stretched and enriched their minds and imaginations. They could do so, however prudently and cautiously, behind the white interpretations of the Scriptures to the God who redeemed people out of the land of bondage.

The authority of the black class leaders rested, however, not only upon their possession of some education, but upon their moral leadership as well. There was, for example, Castile Selby, who was a black Methodist class leader during the entire first half of the nineteenth century. William Capers in writing to a friend said of Selby:

> The weight and force of his character was made up of humility, sincerity, simplicity, integrity and consistency, for all of which he was remarkable, not only among his followers of the colored society of Charleston, but I might say among all whom I have ever known. He was one of those honest men who need no proof of it. No one who ever saw him would suspect him. Disguise or equivocation lurked nowhere about him. Just what he seemed to be, that he invariably was—neither less nor more. Add to this a thorough piety, which was the root and stock of his virtues, and you find elements enough for the character of no common man.

John Mathews was a leader with Catto at the Second Presbyterian Church, a free man and a tailor who died one month before the first shots were fired on Fort Sumter. "His end was peaceful and triumphant," wrote his white pastor. "He was one of the most pious men I ever knew. His love for Jesus was remarkable. He was not an ordinary man: courteous, tender-hearted, dignified, a noble specimen of a coloured Christian."[13]

One of the responsibilities of the leaders for their classes was to see after the needs of any who were poor or infirm. Most of the churches had a "Poor Fund" which was used for this purpose. If a leader discovered a class member in need, he would recommend to the minister or the white officers of the church that a weekly stipend be granted. If approved, it was generally the responsibility of the leader to deliver the stipend and any other help that might be available. At the Circular Congregational Church an average of $375.00 a year was distributed to the needy members of the congregation, who generally totaled around ten. Approximately half of these were black and half white, with the deacons seeing after the needs of the white members. In addition to the small stipend, "fine warm clothing and nourishment" were also furnished. The funds for the stipends came from special weekly collections to which both whites and blacks contributed and not from the regular pew rent which went for the maintenance of the church. Thomas Small, one of the black leaders of the Circular Church, led the other black members in the formation of the "Euphrat Society" which supervised the upkeep of the church's cemetery for blacks and helped to provide for the needs of the poor. In some congregations, blacks had special poor funds which they maintained out of their own meager resources and administered themselves. They were all attempts by blacks to provide some economic support to one another. As such, they were an important means of helping to build solidarity and order in the black community of Charleston.[14]

Black leaders, however, were concerned not only about the physical needs of their class members but about their spiritual and moral life as well. They were careful to note any who were being negligent in their attendance at class meetings or church services and to admonish them to be more faithful. If a class member were involved in a dispute, the leader sought to settle it, and if he could not he took the case to the minister or the white officers of the church. Of particular concern were cases of "gross immorality" that involved such acts as public drunkenness or adultery. In these cases the leader often acted as the public prosecutor, presenting the charges and the evidence before the white session or other church court. If the accused either confessed or was found guilty, the result was generally a suspension from the communion of the church for a year or two. If, however, the convicted one was also impenitent, a complete excommunication was pronounced. In this manner the blacks were subject to the church discipline which was expected of all church members— black and white alike. There was, however, no question about who the rule makers were and in whom final authority rested. Here as elsewhere whites were in control. Their concerns about a narrow personal morality and piety were reflected in the discipline of black church members which, not incidentally, was thought to help make better slaves.[15]

At the Circular Congregational Church, for example, black leaders were zealous to guard the purity of the church and to keep it free from any public scandal. They reported a variety of charges against black members and formal trials would follow. When Betsy Snierlie was found to be living with a man who was not her husband, she was excommunicated. When Jonas Bird, one of the leaders, was himself convicted of seducing and committing adultery with a class member, he was excommunicated. At the same time white members were being disciplined or excommunicated for going to the theater or balls, for public drunkenness, questionable business transactions, and adultery. One white member was admonished for breaking an engagement to a young lady of the city in an imprudent manner and Mr. Robert Pillans, "having lived in an unlawful manner with a colored woman for some time past," and having appeared and made his confession before the white male members, was excommunicated from the church "in view of his criminality and sin."[16]

In spite of the influence of whites in these manners of discipline, it is also clear that the blacks were very serious about it, that the discipline reflected important aspects of their own beliefs, and that blacks were able to use it to strengthen their own community. This was particularly true in regard to fidelity in marriage. Already by 1821 the record books of the Charleston churches reveal that fidelity was an important aspect of slave belief and culture which, no doubt, went far back into their history. In the Methodist churches where blacks had the largest numbers and greatest independence in Charleston, blacks were, from the earliest available church records, frequently disciplined for infidelity. That there were such frequent cases is not surprising in the midst of the chaos of slavery. What is surprising is the seriousness with which slaves took these cases and the consistent discipline they brought to bear on them. It was first and foremost the blacks themselves and their leaders who reported and initiated action on these cases.[17]

III

The black class leaders of the churches in Charleston with their concern for the physical and moral welfare of their members provided, as did those in Liberty County, at least some sense of hope and direction to a people held in bondage. While there is no indication that any of them were ever revolutionaries like the Reverend Nat Turner, except for a few said to be involved with Denmark Vesey, they were the leaders of their people, providing some relief from the cruel realities of slavery. For this very reason, however, they were regarded by the white community with both respect and suspicion. They were respected for their piety and for their role in maintaining order and moral discipline among black church members. Yet they were suspect precisely because they were leaders of a people who should have no leaders, because they spoke with authority among a people who should have no authority, and because they worked allegiance among a people who should have no allegiance except to masters or mistresses.

Some of the free black leaders in Charleston found that they could not remain in the city because of this suspicion and the repressive atmosphere of a slave society. Some went to the North and others joined the black colonists in Liberia. Thomas Catto, the leader at the Second Presbyterian Church, finally decided that he must go North, and after studying for awhile at a Presbyterian seminary became pastor of a black Presbyterian church in Washington, D.C. Boston Drayton, a leader at St. John's Lutheran Church, went with the blessings of John Bachman to Liberia as a Lutheran missionary. There he would serve as governor of one of the states and later as Chief Justice of the Supreme Court of Liberia.[18]

One of the earliest and most famous free black leaders to leave Charleston was Morris Brown. He had been a leader and black preacher in the Methodist church in Charleston during the period (1805–1822) when blacks first began flocking to the Methodist churches in the city. Up until 1815 the black Methodists of Charleston had been allowed their own Quarterly Conference, and their collections, taken up by their leaders, were held and distributed by them. All church trials were also conducted entirely among the blacks with no interference from the whites. In 1815, however, the white Methodists began to claim what they said was a neglected authority over all the affairs of the blacks. The black Quarterly Conferences were abolished and church finances and trials placed under the control of whites. There was considerable opposition from among the blacks, who laid careful plans for forming their own separate church. Morris Brown, Henry Drayton, Amos Cruckshank, and Marcus Brown, all free blacks, journeyed to Philadelphia where they met with Richard Allen and other leaders of the newly formed African Methodist Church. Morris Brown was made an elder and the other black Charlestonians were elected to the office of deacon. Returning to Charleston, they waited for an opportunity to separate from the white Methodists. When a hearse house was built against the

wishes of the blacks on their burial lot on Pitts Street, nearly
every leader delivered up his class papers and 4,367 blacks withdrew from the Methodist churches to form the African Methodist
Episcopal Church of Charleston. They named it Emmanuel,
"God with us." It immediately represented a center of influence
in the new black denomination, being second only to Philadelphia in numbers and wealth. With Morris Brown as their preacher
they succeeded in erecting a neat church building at the corner
of Reid and Hanover Streets which, undoubtedly, became the
focal point of black activities in Charleston. (In addition, class
meetings were evidently held in houses on Anson Street, Cow
Alley, and in Hampstead.) From 1818 to 1822 Morris Brown and
other free black leaders traveled to Philadelphia or Baltimore for
the conferences of the AME Church and firmly established themselves in positions of leadership in the rapidly growing denomination.[19]

Charleston whites were less than pleased with this display of
independence by the African Church. Complaints were filed in
1817 that the worship services were a nuisance and 469 blacks
were arrested. Although they were all discharged, it was a clear
warning: whites wanted no independent black church as a breed-
ing ground for rebellion. The next year as the blacks gathered for
worship on a June morning, the city guards appeared and arrested 140 including Morris Brown and the other leaders of the
church. The following day the city council sentenced Brown and
four others to one month's imprisonment or to give security that
they would leave the state. They chose jail. In order to avoid this
harassment, the church presented in 1820 a petition to the legislature to recognize their right to worship. The petition was
referred to the Charleston delegation, which recommended its
rejection. With this victory, the white authorities in Charleston
moved quickly to tear down the church building that the blacks
had labored with such difficulty to raise.[20]

By January of 1821, almost 3,000 blacks had once again joined
the Methodist churches in the city. They were divided into seventy different classes that met not only in the city but on James

Island, at the Team Boat Ferry on the Ashley, and at several places along Goose Creek. Many of the old watchmen such as Peter Bennet, Castile Selby, and Richard Holloway assumed their former positions as class leaders. Yet not one of the men ordained in the AME church returned. Morris Brown, Henry Drayton, Amos Cruckshank, Charles Carr—they all remained in the African Church and sought to keep it alive. Over 1,400 of their members apparently stayed with them and among their number was Denmark Vesey.[21]

The discovery on June 8, 1822, of the Vesey plot brought a swift end to the African Church. While a clear connection was never established between the church and the intended rebellion —the accounts of the accused varied—there was enough suspicion and near hysteria in the white community to put an end to any large gatherings of blacks for whatever purposes. Thirty-six blacks were executed including several said to be leaders in the AME church. Morris Brown was lucky to escape, with the help of a prominent white, with his life. He joined Richard Allen in Philadelphia where he was soon made a bishop in the AME church.[22]

There were other free black leaders who, with Morris Brown, left Charleston for Philadelphia. There was Charles Carr who had entered the ministry as a black Methodist preacher when he was only sixteen and had labored in and around Charleston for twenty-three years before he went to Philadelphia, and Henry Drayton who had been, with Richard Allen, one of the original founders of the denomination. And there was London Turpin and his friend Marcus Brown. Turpin had been bought from his master, Foster Burnet, in 1813 and freed the next day by Morris Brown his new owner. Marcus Brown had gained his freedom in a similar manner: captured in Africa, sold into slavery, he had earned his freedom with the help of Morris Brown, whose name he apparently adopted. In 1822 he moved with his benefactor to Philadelphia where he became a preacher among the blacks of the city "telling his story with great power." Morris Brown and his friends were joined several years later by Daniel Payne, who after the closing of his school in Charleston, studied for two years at Gettysburg Lutheran Seminary and then went on to become a bishop with Brown in the AME Church. Although a Methodist leader in Charleston, he had been a protege of John Bachman's whose influence had secured his admission to Gettysburg Seminary. Payne would serve as President of Wilberforce University for thirteen years and would make, following the Civil War, an extensive tour of Britain in a quest for financial aid for black schools. Both Payne and Brown would in later years have black colleges named for them. They were, without a doubt, the most influential of the early black church leaders in Charleston.[23]

IV

When the black leaders finished with their classes on Sunday mornings, they and their class members went into the church sanctuaries where white ministers led in worship, preached, and administered the sacraments. Here there were carefully specified places for blacks to sit. These arrangements they generally accepted—but not always.

The most common practice was for the churches to designate the balconies or the galleries as the place for blacks. Such a careful separation of whites and blacks in their seating arrangements served as a reminder that masters and slaves each had their "marked and distinctive place" in the churches as well as in the other areas of southern society.[24]

The seating arrangements at St. John's Lutheran Church were typical of what was found in the churches of Charleston. The north balcony was reserved for blacks until, under the care of John Bachman, their numbers grew to such an extent that it was necessary for the unrented pews in the white section of the balcony to be turned over to the blacks. Some of the free blacks rented, as did the whites, their own pews. They were desirous, said the Minutes of the Congregation, "of procuring for them-

selves and families permanent seats," and were "willing to contribute to the support of the church."[25]

Sometimes open conflicts developed between black and
white members over the right of blacks to claim certain areas
for their own use. At the Circular Church, blacks stood or
were seated in back pews until their numbers began to crowd
the whites and the "corporation ruled they were no longer to
do so, and seats provided in the gallery." At Bethel Methodist
Church a serious schism developed when blacks claimed certain pews as their own and some white members sought to
have the blacks removed. As the black membership of Bethel
had grown, panels or "boxes" had been built in the back of
the church to accomodate the blacks who could not find seats
in the crowded balcony. When the white congregation was
still small, "a few of the older free persons of color were accustomed to take their seats beyond the boxes in the body of
the church; and what was conceded as a privilege, was finally
claimed by them as a right. Gradually others among the colored people began also to pass the barrier of the boxes, and
their boundaries were finally so much enlarged as to encroach
seriously upon the comfort of the whites." A committee was
formed from among the whites to preserve order, and when
on a crowded Sunday morning some of the blacks refused to
vacate their seats for the whites, they were forcibly ejected
from the church. The next Sunday the same thing happened
again. These events caused a serious division in the church
with a number of both blacks and whites leaving to join other
denominations.[26]

When the worship services began, the order of worship reflected the traditions of the particular denominations. In the
Episcopal churches, blacks and whites joined together in the
formal ritual of the Prayer Book. In the Presbyterian, Congregational, and Lutheran churches, the emphasis was on the long,
carefully reasoned sermon, while in the Baptist and Methodist
churches the atmosphere was less formal and the approach more

direct. In all the churches, however, the services had a certain order and decorum that were sometimes missing in the rural churches of the South.[27]

The hymns that were sung were generally of European origin. Those of Watts and Wesley were in most of the hymnals as were older hymns and tunes. In all probability Negro spirituals were rarely if ever sung during the morning worship services of the Charleston churches. Whites generally disapproved of them (they had, after all, good reasons to be suspicious!) and even some of the black leaders such as Daniel Payne found them distasteful.[28]

This did not mean, however, that the blacks did not contribute significantly to the music of the churches. On the contrary, their singing was a vital part of the worship services. When in 1818 they withdrew from the Methodist churches to form their own African Methodist Episcopal Church, their singing was keenly missed. "None but those who are accustomed to attend the churches of Charleston, with their crowded galleries, can well appreciate the effect of such an immense withdrawal," wrote the Methodist minister F. A. Mood. "The galleries, hitherto crowded, were almost completely deserted, and it was a vacancy that could be *felt*. The absence of their responses and hearty songs was really felt to be a loss to those so long accustomed to hearing them." Forty years later when a new church building was dedicated in Charleston, a writer would report in a church paper "You have doubtless heard . . . sublime music in the house of God; but if you never heard Old Hundred, Mear, and Coronation, sung by two thousand blacks, . . . you have yet to learn what an engine music can be made for lifting the soul above this earth on which we stand."[29]

The sermons which the white Charleston ministers preached to their mixed congregations were generally carefully prepared in book-lined studies. Their topics would range from "Infant Baptism, A Gospel Ordinance" to "The Voice of God in Calamity—or Reflections on the Loss of the Steam-Boat Home" and "Sermons Preached on the Occasion of the Great Charleston Fire of

1838." While carefully prepared sermons were the general rule, the Methodist and Baptist sermons were no doubt of a simpler style, providing a greater appeal to the largely illiterate blacks of the city. Two Methodist ministers, William Capers and W. M. Wightman, joined in 1845 in making a plea for preaching that would reach black slaves as well as white masters. It is not a "valid objection that the coloured people are illiterate," they declared. "Preaching ought to be plain, that it may be in demonstration of the Spirit and of power. And least of all might we make allowance for that vile abuse of preaching which affects excellency of speech with a jargon of high-sounding nonsense."[30]

At the Second Presbyterian Church, Thomas Smyth preached sermons that reflected the style of most of the other ministers in the city—they were long and logical. Never one to cut himself short, Smyth found that his family had devised many ways to let him know he had preached long enough. A speaking tube connected the pulpit with the choir loft. Through this, Fleetwood Lanneau, the violinist, attempted to signal him that it was time to stop, and although it could be heard by the people in the front pews the signal was usually ignored. One of the men of the congregation next volunteered to put his hat in the aisle, but this too failed. Smyth's sons tried to check him: one would cough from the choir loft to stop the sermon and another would cough from the family pew to stop the pastoral prayer at ten minutes. It was all to no avail. In spite of their length, however, his sermons attracted many people with a number of both whites and blacks joining the church.[31]

V

High points in the slave's sabbath were the sacraments of baptism and communion. Perhaps more than any other public event in ante-bellum Charleston, these sacraments served to lift the spirits of an oppressed people and to call into question the proud claims of white owners.

Looking down from the balconies of fine old Charleston chruches, black men and women could see their friends and children being baptized; they could see them passing through the waters of the Red Sea, dying and rising with Jesus, becoming a part of the visible community of Christ's people. During his years at St. John's Lutheran Church, John Bachman would baptize more than two thousand blacks. Some would come as adults to kneel and be washed by the baptismal waters. Others would come as infants in the arms of their slave parents, unknowing recipients of bondage and grace, to feel Bachman's hand upon their heads and to hear him say, "I baptize thee in the name of the Father, and the Son, and the Holy Ghost."[32]

At the Episcopal and Roman Catholic churches, blacks, both free and slave, would often serve as godparents. Whites, however, would sometimes join with black parents to stand beside them as sponsors or godparents for the slave child. Julia Ann, an infant daughter of Thomas (a slave of Mr. Smith) and Hetty (a slave of Mr. William Patton) was brought forward by her parents to be baptized by the Episcopal minister Paul Trapier with Mrs. Patton standing as godmother and William Cheeseborough as godfather. Turning to the white godparents, Trapier inquired if the child had already been baptized. Then after prayer and Scripture reading, the godparents were asked if they renounced "the devil and all his works, the vain pomp and glory of the world, with all covetous desires of the same, and the sinful desires of the flesh," so that they would not follow or be led by them. "I renounce them all," they responded, "and, by God's help, will endeavor not to follow, nor be led by them." Having made these promises, the white godparents were asked "wilt thou also on thy part take heed that this child learn the Creed, the Lord's Prayer, and the Ten Commandments, and all other things which a Christian ought to know and believe to his soul's health?" "I will by God's help," they said. "Wilt thou take heed that this child, so soon as sufficiently instructed, be brought to the Bishop to be confirmed by him?" They answered, "I will, God being my helper."[33]

At the First Baptist Church, great numbers of blacks were immersed in the baptismal waters before gathered congregations of blacks and whites. Renouncing their sins and putting their trust in Jesus, they were plunged beneath the cleansing waters to emerge as new persons in Christ and members of the First Baptist Church of Charleston. In recognition of their new status, the congregation of whites and blacks came forward to extend to the baptized slaves the right hand of Christian fellowship. From that moment they were addressed as sister or brother and their names were so listed in the church records.[34]

For these blacks who had been baptized and received into the fellowship of Charleston churches, the way was open to participate in the sacrament of the Lord's Supper. This sacrament was for Protestant Christians an outward and visible sign of their union to Christ and their mutual love and fellowship with each other as members of the same mystical body. In the words of Jones' catechism, the Supper shows to all the world the "death of Christ for sin."[35]

On communion Sundays at the First (Scots) Presbyterian Church, black slaves sitting in the balcony could look down on long communion tables with benches on both sides. Set in the center aisle of the sanctuary and along the front of the church, the tables had on them silver tankards, chalices, and bread trays all covered with a white cloth. Those blacks and whites who would receive the Lord's Supper held communion tokens which indicated, in a practice that went back to the Church of Scotland, that they were ready to receive the sacraments. A preparatory service had been held on Saturday to distribute the tokens to those who wished to receive communion and whose lives during the past months had exhibited Christian piety and discipline. There were two identical sets of tokens—a silver set for whites and a pewter set for blacks. On one side of the tokens was a representation of the communion table, cup, and tray with the words, "This do in remembrance of Me," and on the other side there was the seal of the Church of Scotland.[36]

When the time came to receive communion the white members who were to participate came forward. After they were seated at the table, they gave their tokens to the elders who distributed the bread and the wine. Then the blacks came down from the balcony to the same Lord's Table. There they handed over their tokens to their leaders and received from them the bread and wine from the same silver trays and chalices. Having received the Holy Supper, they remained seated at the Lord's Table, in the midst of the white slaveholders and in the center of the church, until the conclusion of a final meditation.[37]

VI

Sunday afternoons in Charleston often provided an opportunity for slave weddings and sometimes were the occasion of a slave funeral. These events reflected both the pathos of a slave's life and black people's quest for personal dignity in the midst of the terrible forces that surrounded their lives and kept them in bondage. The weddings, which were sanctioned by the churches but not the state, were a time for festivity, yet they appeared to have a certain somber air about them. The funerals were a time for grief, yet they often contained a clear note of celebration and release from the sorrows of slavery.

Black weddings were generally held in one of several places— some were in churches, some were in ministers' homes, and some were in the homes of masters or mistresses. The church weddings were often in "the presence of many witnesses," both blacks and whites. For the blacks it was an opportunity not only to dress in their finest clothes which far exceeded, according to many reports, the plain clothes of plantation slaves, but also to claim with their clothes and their vows their own humanity and commitment to one another. For the whites it was a strange and awkward situation, for the weddings presented a conflict in convictions which they could never completely reconcile: the necessity of marriage and the legitimacy of slavery.[38]

Before the marriage of slaves could take place, the owners had to give their consent. Sometimes they refused. Martha, a member of the First Baptist Church, was excommunicated for living with a man who was not her husband. She would have married him except for the objections of her mistress.[39] It appears, however, at least from church records, that in Charleston the owners often gave their consent.

Jack, a slave of Mrs. Campbell, was married by Paul Trapier to Charlotte, a slave of the Misses Ramsey, at the Ramsey home on Broad Street. The owners had given their consent and were there for the wedding. In the presence of God and these owners, Trapier asked Jack and Charlotte the familiar vows of the Episcopal wedding service:

> Jack, wilt thou have this woman to be thy wedded wife, to live together after God's ordinance in the holy estate of Matrimony? Wilt thou love her, comfort her, honour, and keep her in sickness and in health, and, forsaking all others, keep thee only unto her, so long as ye both shall live?

Jack responded, "I will" as did Charlotte when Trapier addressed the vow to her. "Who giveth this Woman to be married to this Man?" asked Trapier. In all probability it was Charlotte's owner who took her hand and placed it in the minister's joining it with Jack's. Holding her hand, Jack repeated after Trapier,

> I Jack take thee Charlotte to be my wedded Wife, to have and to hold from this day forward, for better for worse, for richer for poorer, in sickness and in health, to love and to cherish, till death do us part, according to God's holy ordinance; and thereto I plight thee my troth.

"I Charlotte take thee Jack . . ." responded Charlotte.

"Those whom God hath joined together," declared Trapier, "let no man put asunder."[40]

When death came to end the life of a slave and bring release from a world of sorrows, the funeral service was an occasion when hope could be expressed for a better future hid in the mystery and grace of God. The black person whose past had been cut off by the slave ship and auction block and whose present had been restricted and corrupted by the toils and bonds of slavery, placed great emphasis upon the funeral. It was a "rite of passage" that all people must face, yet for many slaves it was more. It represented for many the one hope for a transition from bondage to freedom, from death to life. "Want, want!" exclaimed the dying black man, John Boquet, when asked by William Capers if he wanted anything. "Glory be to God, I am done with want for ever! Want! Want! I know no want but heaven, and I am almost there by the blood of Jesus."[41]

In order to insure decent funerals for themselves, the blacks of Charleston ran the risk of forming their own funeral societies or "bands." Although whites tolerated these bands, they were always suspicious and frequently denounced them as secret and possibly dangerous. The two outstanding exceptions were the Brown Fellowship Society and the Humane Brotherhood. The Brown Fellowship, the better known of the two, had been organized in 1790 by "free brown men, natives of the city of Charleston" and had as its purpose the establishment of a fund to relieve its members "in the hour of their distresses, sickness and death." Its members included the wealthiest of the free "persons of color" in Charleston, such as the DeReefs, Kinlocks, and Holloways. In 1794 the Society purchased a lot on Pitts Street for use as a cemetery. It lay next to the burial ground of Bethel Methodist Church and was consecrated by the pastor of a number of the society's members—the Rev. Thomas Frost, rector of St. Philip's Episcopal Church. A single-story frame building was erected on the southwest corner of the lot as a society hall. The membership of the Brown Fellowship, however, was so conservative and was so preoccupied with maintaining the status of its own members in the black society of Charleston that it was viewed with a complacent and satisfied eye by the city authorities. Careful minutes of every meeting were kept and were occasionally reviewed by whites. A neat volume of the Society's *Rules and Regulations* giving a history of the

Fellowship and a list of the members was even published in 1844 by a Charleston printer.

The Humane Brotherhood was composed of the darker skinned "Free Dark Men of Colour" and had the same general purposes as the Brown Fellowship. Their burial grounds lay side by side and were separated by a neat fence.[42]

The other black burial societies were not, however, viewed by white authorities with such calm assurance as they were not convinced that their Societies were focused on "the world to come." "Many associations, under the general title of 'Bands,' have been found to exist among the colored people," declared a report to the city in 1850, and "there is reason to believe, that these associations have, in *some instances,* been perverted from their original or ostensible object. . . ." In order to counteract the influence of the bands, some of the churches of the city threatened disciplinary action against any church member who belonged to one. In the Methodist churches, a black leader could not continue in office if he belonged to "any such association," and no black person in connection with one would receive the support and protection of the church. These regulations, however, appear to have been of little use and there is no indication that any disciplinary action was ever brought against a black church member for belonging to a band.[43]

More effective in counteracting the influence of the bands were the efforts by the churches to provide their black members with funeral services and proper burials. Most of the churches had their own "colored burial ground"—a place set apart from the white cemeteries so that even in death blacks might be kept in their "place." Paul Trapier, for example, buried blacks in a number of different cemeteries. Andrew Jervey was buried in "the ground of the colored people of St. Michael's Church," Primers Hayne in the "yard of colored people of St. Peter's Church," and Sambo White in the "ground of Calvary Episcopal Church." By 1856 there were fifteen "colored cemeteries" in Charleston: two were owned by the city, one belonged to the Brown Fellowship Society and the Humane Brotherhood, and the remainder were owned by white churches.[44]

In the Methodist churches black leaders who had received written permission from the presiding elder were allowed to conduct funeral services. A large section of the Bethel cemetery on Pitts Street had been set aside for the black members of the church. Following the practice of the plantations, funerals were often held on Sunday or at night so that those who could not get away from their work could attend. Funerals were held here "sometimes every night in the week," complained a white critic who claimed that "three or four hundred negroes and a tumultuous crowd of other slaves" made so much noise that they disturbed the whole neighborhood. "It appears to be a jubilee for every slave in the city," he declared, while warning: "let it be remembered too that the officiating priests are black men."[45]

At the Second Presbyterian Church, careful rules were established for the use of the "burying ground for our colored people" which was three miles from the church at a settlement called Rikerville. A master or mistress could purchase for $5.00 a single plot "for his or her servant" or for $15.00 could buy a plot eight feet square as "a servants' family burial ground." Any colored member of the church who paid down $3.00 and made a 12 1/2¢ monthly payment was entitled to an eight foot square plot "for them and their children." Strangers could have a plot for $11.00 while destitute black members of the church could be buried free of all charges.[46]

When a black member of the Second Presbyterian Church died, Thomas Smyth would usually conduct the funeral service in the church itself. The service would consist of Scripture reading and prayer, hymns and a meditation—probably reflecting on the brevity of life and the hopes of the righteous for heaven. After the funeral service, the church's hearse would carry the body to the colored burial ground. Here a black leader would take charge of the burial service. A grave would have been opened by the sexton, Francis Dent, who was one of the black leaders and who had charge of collecting the burial fees and providing a general oversight of the cemetery. When the body was lowered into the grave, Maum Cinda, the assistant sexton, would "snatch a fearful joy" from casting the first handful of earth on the coffin of the one who had crossed over the Jordan into the Promised Land. Frederick Law Olmsted, the northern traveler through the South, may very well have been observing this scene which he described on his visit to Charleston: the service was "simple and decorous" and was conducted by a "well-dressed and dignified elderly negro" who used the Presbyterian order. "The grave was filled by the negroes, before the crowd, which was quite large, dispersed. Beside myself, only one white man, probably a policeman, was in attendance."[47]

When the setting sun brought to an end the slave's sabbath, blacks of Charleston turned homeward walking the sand and cobblestone streets past fine churches and elegant homes to the cramped and enclosed slave quarters and the shanties of Charleston Neck. Whatever freedom had been experienced on this day of rest, whatever human dignity had been found in the rites and sacraments of the church, whatever dreams had been stirred by Christian hope and charity, now faced the loneliness and terror of a slave's night. Here the paternalism of the whites faded and the cruel forces of the human heart emerged in the tyranny of an oppressive system. The slave's sabbath had not brought an end to slavery—only a little rest, some joy and a struggling, faithful company of believers.

8

A Charleston Zion

I

John Adger, recently returned from mission work in Armenia, sat listening to one of the long sermons of Thomas Smyth. Above him in the galleries of the Second Presbyterian Church sat black men and women looking down on the white parishioners gathered below. Adger turned and looked up at them. There was Harriet Johnson, the best singer in the church, and Francis Dent, the sexton, and his wife Betsy who was a slave of the Adgers. Maum Cinda was here as were the leaders Thomas Catto and Johnson, Mitchell, and Matthews. And there were the others who crowded the galleries and who for Adger were a nameless mass of black slaves. "Who are these people?" thought Adger, and how far does Smyth's "preaching to his white congregation" go over their heads?[1]

Adger was convinced that a new work among the blacks was needed in Charleston. While in Armenia he had translated Charles Jones' catechism and he knew all about Jones' missionary labors among the black slaves of Liberty County. What was needed in Charleston, he thought, was an urban missionary to black slaves, one whose ministry would focus on the urban slave as Jones' had focused on the plantation slave. Unlike the ministers of the Charleston churches who gave most of their time to their white members, a home missionary could direct all of his teaching and preaching efforts to the blacks of the city.[2]

It was clear to Adger that not only Christian duty but a prudent regard for the interests of the South demanded that the southern churches give greater attention to the black slaves. Forces outside the South were increasing their attacks on both slavery and the churches in the South. "Our domestic institutions," declared Adger's friend James Henley Thornwell, "can be maintained against the world if we but allow Christianity to throw its broad shield over them. But if we so act as to array the Bible against our social economy, then our social economy must fall."[3]

On his return from Armenia in 1846, Adger had stopped in London, and there he had met Smyth who was vacationing in Great Britain. Together they had experienced the assaults of abolitionists. They had heard Southerners denounced for holding blacks in a cruel slavery, for refusing to evangelize them, and for keeping the Bible and religious instruction from them.[4]

Charleston and her ministers had been the focal point of attacks by evangelical abolitionists in Britain. Two years before Adger and Smyth had met in London, Smyth had been instrumental in raising money in Charleston to aid the Free Church of Scotland, which had withdrawn from the Church of Scotland because of state interference in the life of the kirk. This action, with its voluntary abandonment of state support, had been regarded by many American Protestants as a heroic move in the cause of religious freedom. A public meeting had been called in Charleston and Smyth had been asked to deliver a discourse on "the claims of the Free Church of Scotland to the sympathy and assistance of American Christians." In his address, Smyth had praised the Scottish people for their long struggle for "liberty of conscience, liberty of opinion, and liberty of action." Then turning to his Charleston audience he had declared:

The appeal addresses us, as Americans. To us as the friends of liberty and human rights, and the noble champions of civil and religious freedom, does the Free Church of Scotland look for sympathy, encouragement, and aid in this noble effort to better our example.

The white Charleston audience has been enthralled. When Smyth was finished, they had enthusiastically responded by raising over two thousand dollars. The address had been published and sent with the money to the Free Church, which received it gratefully.[5]

British abolitionists, however, had been quick to point out the self-deception and cruel irony in receiving, in the name of freedom, money from Charleston, South Carolina. "This is one of the coolest of many cool productions," declared a Glasgow editor, "of those in the Southern States, called ministers of Christ, who prate away, *ad nauseam,* on the unbounded freedom enjoyed under the American Constitution. . . . Ministers of Christ!!!" he exclaimed. "Servants, and willing ones, too, of Satan, would be a more fitting designation." There could be no unity with slaveholders, nor could the Free Church accept "blood-stained money, wrung by the gory whip from poor, oppressed, down trodden slaves."[6]

"Send back the money" became the cry of the abolitionists. Frederick Douglass, the greatest of the black American abolitionists, described the scene he found on visiting Edinburg: " 'Send back the money!' in large capitals stared from every street corner: 'Send back the money!' was the chorus of the popular street songs; 'send back the money!' was the heading of the leading editorials in the daily newspapers." Smyth's name was painted on the walls and pavements of Glasgow and "send back the money" was smeared in blood-red paint on Free Church buildings. A long letter from Lewis Tappan and other anti-slavery men in America was fired off denouncing the Free Church for accepting the money and demanding that it be returned. William Lloyd Garrison filled the *Liberator,* the leading abolitionist paper in America, with denunciations and with reports of the growing uproar in

Britain. Douglass reported from Scotland that "public meeting succeeded public meeting, speech after speech, pamphlet after pamphlet, editorial after editorial, sermon after sermon, lashed the conscientious Scotch people into a perfect furor."[7]

When Smyth arrived in Britain for his vacation, he was immediately challenged to debate Douglass or one of the other American abolitionists. He refused and in the process raised questions about the character and reputation of the American abolitionists. The response of the Scottish Anti-Slavery Society was a cry of outrage and indignation: the American abolitionists were known and well respected in Britain, but Smyth came from Charleston, South Carolina, and was the reputed defender and ally of man-stealers. "You are *accused*," they told Smyth,

> of being the enemy of our race—of being identified with, if not yourself actually guilty of, crimes the most dreadful and heaven daring of which men on earth can be guilty . . . forget not that you come from *Charleston, South Carolina*—the land where men and women are degraded to the level of brutes—where the prerogative of God is invaded and where an interdict is put upon the Commission of the Saviour to preach the gospel to *every creature*—where the laws of the Eternal One are trampled openly under foot and where *might* and not *right* is the rule of actions for persons who claim to be the followers of Jesus Christ. . . .[8]

Adger felt the fury of these attacks when he joined Smyth in London to attend the first meeting of the Evangelical Alliance. Here, with such prominent American churchmen as Lyman Beecher and Robert Baird, they joined with evangelical leaders in Britain and the continent in the formation of an alliance which would express their unity and provide an opportunity for co-operating in the task of evangelizing the world. Slavery, however, had almost immediately become a divisive issue. The British and American abolitionists demanded that those from slaveholding states not be allowed to participate in the Alliance. In the debates that followed, Smyth and Adger heard their Christian convictions questioned and their Southern homeland denounced. It was a bitter experience and brought home to them the growing isolation of the South. While the Alliance eventually refused to bar those from the slave holding states and while the Free Church never sent the money back to Charleston, the British churches began to declare that they would no longer have Christian fellowship with slaveholders or their churches. This increasing isolation helped to awaken in both Smyth and Adger the painful awareness that there was a need for a new and more comprehensive work among the blacks. If the Protestant churches of the South were to claim a place among evangelical churches, they must at least be able to show that they were concerned about the religious instruction of the black slaves in their midst. Accused and isolated, southern churchmen would increasingly turn to the religious instruction of slaves as part of their desperate attempt to justify human bondage to an indignant world.[9]

II

Adger's plan for a new approach was to organize, as Smyth's associate at the Second Presbyterian Church, a new church for the blacks of Charleston. The blacks would meet in the Presbyterian Lecture Hall on Society Street until their own building could be raised. They were to remain members of the Second Church under the direction of the white session, but they were to have their own building and Adger as their minister would direct his preaching and his efforts in religious instruction solely toward them.[10]

Just as Charles Jones was a missionary to the plantation slaves under the sponsorship of the Liberty County Association for the Religious Instruction of Negroes, Adger would be a missionary to city blacks under the sponsorship of the session of the Second Presbyterian Church. He would, like Jones, receive no financial support from the sponsor. What he would receive, like Jones, was the necessary approval and supervision from influential whites which would make his work appear legitimate and acceptable to a suspicious white community.[11]

In May of 1847, Adger's plan was presented to the congregation of the Second Church. Francis H. Elmore, soon to take John C. Calhoun's seat in the United States Senate, presided over the meeting. Adger preached from the text "The poor have the gospel preached unto them." And who, he asked, are the poor of Charleston? They are easily distinguishable he answered:

> They are a class separated from ourselves by their color, their position in society, their relation to our families, their national origin, and their moral, intellectual, and physical condition. Nowhere are the poor so closely and intimately connected with the higher classes as are our poor with us. They belong to us. We also belong to them. They are divided out among us and mingled up with us, and we with them, in a thousand ways. They live with us, eating from the same storehouse, drinking from the same fountains, dwelling in the same enclosures, forming parts of the same families. Our mothers confide us, when infants, to their arms, and sometimes to the very milk of their breasts. Their children are, to some extent, unavoidably the playmates of our childhood—grow up with us under the same roof—sometimes pass through all the changes of life with us, and then, either they stand weeping by our bedsides, or else we drop a tributary tear by theirs, when death comes to close the long connection and to separate the good master and his good servant.
>
> Such, my friends, are those whom we consider the poor of this city. There they are—behold them. See them all around you, in these streets, in all these dwellings; a race distinct from us, yet closely united to us, brought in God's mysterious providence from a foreign land, and placed under our care, and made members of our households. They fill the humblest places of our state of society; they serve us; they give us their strength, yet they are not more truly ours than we are truly theirs. They are our poor—our poor brethren; children of our God and Father; dear to our Savior; to the like of whom he preached; for the like of whom he died, and to the least of whom every act of Christian compassion and kindness which we show he will consider as shown also to himself.[12]

Adger's answer was perhaps the clearest and most eloquent expression of the paternalism that characterized the Charleston churches in their work among the blacks of the city. The system of slavery with all of its terror was accepted without question, and yet the black slaves were seen as spiritual brothers and sisters, as those to whom whites could show the compassion and kindness they owed their Lord.

The idea of a church where blacks would assemble separate from whites, was not, however, greeted with enthusiasm by some. It seemed a dangerous step even though the minister was to be white. Memories of the Denmark Vesey plot with its associations with the black African Methodist Church still troubled the minds of many whites. The editor of the Charleston *Mercury* wrote that the present setup was sufficient and that its agitation was "ill-advised and calculated to evil consequences." A. G. Magrath, writing anonymously as "Many Citizens," expressed even greater alarm. An old schoolmate of Adger's, Magrath would soon become judge of the United States District Court and would serve as governor of South Carolina during the last days of the war. As a fire-eating judge, he would declare that the foreign slave trade was not piracy when the slave ship *Wanderer* was captured illegally selling African slaves in Georgia.[13]

Writing a series of letters to the *Mercury,* Magrath now denounced this whole plan of a new work among the blacks. Instead of simply gathering with the whites, Magrath declared the blacks would be joined together in an organized society with the right to consult and deliberate and be heard in matters of church government. They would develop a spiritual allegiance to their church. They would learn that what they suffer for the church will be a proud distinction. They would learn the lessons of zeal, and the glory of martyrdom. "To minds thus matured, what will be the language of the master or the owner?" (It was a vision perhaps already being fulfilled beyond what Magrath feared!)[14]

"Very dreadful indeed!" was the sarcastic reply of James Henley Thornwell, the influential Presbyterian theologian at South Carolina College. "We fear that the nerves of 'Many Citizens' can hardly have recovered even after so long a time, from the severe shock which they must have received from the bare contemplation of all these horrors." Thornwell, writing in Columbia,

thought that "Many Citizens" reflected the "morbidness" of
Charleston on the subject which could be found in "no other city
in the Southern States."[15]

Adger knew only too well the source of this "morbidness," for
he had unforgettable memories of the Denmark Vesey plot. As
a boy of seven he had looked out of a third floor window of his
father's home and seen on King Street a long row of gallows with
Vesey's lieutenant, Gullah Jack, and twenty one other blacks
hanging from them. Adger also knew what few other Charlestonians knew or remembered—that Denmark Vesey had been a respected member of the Second Presbyterian Church. Although
Vesey had been associated, according to witnesses at his trial,
with the African Church, he had in fact joined the Second Church
in April of 1817, at the very time Morris Brown was leading the
blacks out of the Methodist churches to form an independent
black church. Vesey had maintained his membership at Second
Church and there had been little to distinguish him from other
black members. That was what made his memory so dangerous
for the religious instruction of slaves. White ministers like Richard Fuller, Charles Jones, and Thornwell had all been saying that
if Vesey and the other conspirators had been under the influence
of a white minister, there never would have been a plot. But
Vesey had been, in spite of the strange silence of the court records, a member of an established Charleston church with a white
pastor. It had not prevented him from being at the center of the
most dangerous insurrection planned by urban slaves. Replying
to "Many Citizens," Adger nevertheless insisted that in his plans
the blacks would always be under the supervision of whites and
that the need for a new work was desperate. There simply was not
enough room in all of the white churches of Charleston to accommodate the blacks of the city nor was the present religious
instruction sufficient for their needs. These assurances were,
however, not enough to calm the controversy which now became
more intense.[16]

In the meantime, a similar plan was being pursued by some in
the Episcopal Church. Paul Trapier, former minister of St. Mi-

chael's who had been forced to leave apparently because of his high church views, had become interested in organizing a separate church for blacks. Using arguments similar to Adger's, he had persuaded the Diocesan Convention to give its sanction to the work. At first he held services in the basement of the parsonage of St. Philip's Church before moving to a Temperance Hall above a carriage warehouse. Like the Second Church, the erection of a church building was planned. As the walls began to rise, the city became more and more excited. An angry crowd gathered, threatening to pull the walls down. The aristocratic Trapier attributed the trouble to demagogues who incited "the jealousy of white mechanics against the negroes." But before any damage could be done, "influential citizens, jealous for the honor of their city" persuaded the mob to desist, promising to call a public meeting to discuss the whole matter.[17]

When the meeting was held, a Committee of Fifty, made up of the social and political leaders of Charleston, was appointed to investigate the problem and to seek to discover if these new plans for the religious instruction of blacks posed any threat to the white community. James L. Petigru, leading citizen of the city, was named chairman by the mayor. After a long and careful study, the committee reported that as long as a white was in charge who was designated by the authorities of some church and that as long as the meetings were not held in secret or at night without a proper number of whites, the legislature had been "content to leave the field open to the free exercise of missionary zeal." On the motion of C. G. Memminger, future Secretary of the Treasury for the Confederacy, the committee reported to the city that there was no cause for alarm and that the religious instruction of the blacks, "combined with a prudent attention to the preservation of order, is a work highly acceptable . . . and of great advantage to the commonwealth."[18]

With this favorable report, the way was cleared for the new work among the blacks of Charleston to begin in earnest. While this new work would never reach the number of blacks the Methodists alone would reach at Trinity or Bethel, one highly successful congregation would be established, and the new work would be supported by many of the most influential members of the white community. It would be an experiment in paternalism and an attempt to put into practice the aristocratic ideals of the South. It would represent, in fact, the highest example of those ideals as they expressed themselves through the religious life of the South. As such, it was not by chance that this new work was undertaken by the wealthy Episcopal and Presbyterian churches of Charleston.

III

By 1850 Calvary Episcopal Church had been built and was functioning as a separate black church with Trapier as the minister. That same year the Anson Street Presbyterian Church was completed with John Adger as the minister.

The opening service of the Anson Street Church was an occasion of great importance for those whites concerned about the religious instruction of slaves. Charles C. Jones came to participate in the service and lead the congregation in prayer for the new work. James Henley Thornwell came from Columbia (where he was soon to be elected president of the South Carolina College) to preach the opening sermon. Adger and Smyth were, of course, here along with other leading ministers and citizens of the city. "It was felt to be suitable," wrote Adger, that in dedicating a church for the religious instruction of slaves, those involved "should set their views before other Christian slaveholders in the South." It was hoped that this might stimulate interest among Southerners in the work as well as "contribute somewhat to the correction of those world-wide errors which prevailed as to the true character of slavery. . . ." With such a "sensitive subject" as the concern of the evening, it is little wonder that "the congregation that assembled to take part in the dedication of the house to the worship of God by negroes, was composed exclusively of white people." (Charles Jones, not one to let the opportunity pass him by, had already preached that afternoon to the black congregation.)[19]

Thornwell's sermon was on the text, "Masters, give unto your servants that which is just and equal; knowing that you also have a master in heaven." The sermon was perhaps the most comprehensive statement by any southern clergyman on the question of slavery and clearly reflected the presuppositions and ideals of southern paternalism. Thornwell sought to present what he thought was the true nature of slavery and to explain the relationship between master and slave. Basic to Thornwell's argument was his defense of the paternalistic ideal of an ordered and stable society where every person had his or her place. In such a society every right involved a corresponding duty. The right of the master was to the labor of the slave. This Thornwell defended in great detail to the white Charlestonians. In particular he attacked the arguments of Channing and the abolitionists. At the same time, however, Thornwell insisted that the slave also had certain rights which involved "all the essential rights of humanity." These included such temporal rights as the right to acquire knowledge—which though legally denied "is practically admitted" by Southerners—the right of the family, and the right to personal safety. It was the duty of the State to protect these real rights of the slave, and there was a great need for these rights to be "defined by law and enforced by penalties." On the part of masters, one of the highest and most solemn obligations was to "give to the servants, to the utmost extent of their ability, free access to the instruction and institutions of the gospel." The opening of the Anson Street Church, declared Thornwell, was proof that this duty had not been wholly disregarded.[20]

The work at both Anson Street and Calvary was, however, of mixed success. At Calvary there were never more than fifty-five black members, although there were up to six hundred attending Sunday school classes. The work at Calvary reached its peak in numbers in 1856 but declined the next year after Trapier had to resign because of ill-health. At Anson Street, the Sunday school was also the most successful part of the work, with few blacks actually becoming communing members of the church. Neither Trapier, the high churchman, nor Adger, the Old School Presbyterian, seemed to have been particularly well suited for the work. (Adger, however, would receive in 1853 the honorary degree "Doctor of Divinity" from the College of Charleston for his work among the slaves.) Their preaching, though directed solely toward the blacks, never apparently appealed to them and probably remained the "white preaching" to which Adger had objected.[21]

It was only after Adger had resigned in 1852 because of failing eyesight that the attempt to develop a separate church for blacks began to meet with substantial success. In that year John L. Girardeau became the minister at the Anson Street Church. He was a cousin of Charles Jones with family roots deep in Liberty County and Huguenot history. Born on James Island, Girardeau had spent his youth among the island blacks where he was at home with the Gullah dialect. Using his knowledge of the language and utilizing the techniques of a folk preacher, he became immediately popular among the blacks of the city. He used what he called "key-words" when preaching—that is, words he would emphasize through the inflection of his voice and the expression of his face. "Holy God," he said in a tone of humility and awe and "sin hateful" with a look of intense abhorrence. The large crowds which his preaching drew soon made it necessary for the work to be enlarged.[22]

With the urging of Girardeau and Smyth an independent church, no longer under the authority of the session of the Second Church, was organized for blacks by Charleston Presbytery. Over $25,000 was quickly raised for a new church building with most of the funds coming from the Adger and Smyth families. The blacks named the church Zion. Located on Calhoun Street, it was the largest church building in Charleston. A small core of whites belonged (the Adgers were clearly the leaders) and served as officers. This time, however, they were the ones who sat in the gallery and listened to sermons directed primarily to members of another race, for the whole thrust of the church was toward the reaching and nurturing of blacks.[23]

The organization of Zion was in many ways similar to the work which some of the white churches had developed for their black members. The blacks were divided into classes with their own leaders who met with their classes weekly, visited their members, looked after the sick and poor, examined applicants for marriage, conducted funerals, and reported cases requiring discipline. Girardeau, however, sought to extend the work of the leaders and to carry to a logical conclusion the paternalistic ideals of an organic community. The whites at Zion would clearly be the patrons doing for the blacks what the blacks' place in a slave society forbade them to do—govern themselves. "We enter this church," declared the white members in their covenant, "as white members of the same, with the fullest understanding that its primary design and chief purpose is to benefit the coloured and especially the slave population of this city, and that the white membership is a feature added to the original organization for the purpose of better securing the ends of that organization." By accepting and taking seriously their responsibility to be patrons of black slaves, these concerned whites extended their control over the religious life of the slaves who accepted their care and patronage. By their careful and dedicated supervision of the classes, leaders, and activities of the church, the whites of Zion were able to control the religious life of the black members to a degree which no other church in Charleston was able or cared to do.[24]

At the same time, however, the blacks evidently found that they could use this paternalism to their own advantage—Zion was their church as no other church in Charleston had been theirs since Morris Brown and the African Methodist Church. It was a building, a place, that had been built for them. Here they could gather and claim a community and thus a humanity in the very midst of an alienating and dehumanizing bondage. That they could use the paternalism of Zion to their own advantage can be seen both in the continuing suspicion and sometimes open hostility that was found in the white community (Girardeau was nearly lynched in 1859) and in the emergence of the Zion Church as a large and vital black church following the Civil War.[25]

It was in regard to their names, however, that the slave members of Zion showed most clearly that they could use the whites' paternalism to their own advantage. All across the South, whites had denied that slaves had surnames. In Liberty County there had been Sam and Toney, Tenah and Niger, but no surnames had been acknowledged. If a surname were given as a means of identification, it was the name of the slave's owner. This practice was a means of emphasizing that slaves had, from a white perspective, no lasting family connections: slaves were the property of whites, not members of a black family with a name. At best, slaves were regarded as "servants," "children" of paternal white masters or mistresses and therefore bearers of their names. For slaves to claim surnames was thus a means of rejecting the pretentions of their owners, but for slaves to do so publicly would have been a bold display of independence. At Zion, however, they did precisely this.[26]

The rolls of the Charleston churches tell the story. In the early part of the nineteenth century, when the ideals of the American Revolution had raised questions even in Charleston about slavery, slaves were simply listed with surnames—probably the same as their present owners. By 1821 the Methodists had begun to list those blacks coming back into their membership from the African Church with a little telltale +: Peter+Bennett, Paul+Todd, Jacob+Belser. Following the Denmark Vesey plot, however, a change took place. From now on slaves were listed without a surname, only a Christian name and the designation "servant of . . .": "London, servant of Tho. Bennett," "Judy, servant of Col. I. Bryan." This practice continued in the Charleston churches until the conclusion of the Civil War. At Zion, however, blacks were able to use the space provided by paternalistic whites to claim publicly their own family names. Edward Jones, the white clerk of the session at Zion, recorded not only the owners of hundreds of slaves who joined Zion, but the surnames of the slaves as well. Over 85% of the slaves who joined Zion gave surnames different from that of their current owners. After 1857, the percentage was even more remarkable: of the 303 slaves who joined Zion after that date, 279 gave their own surnames and not that of their owners. Not only did they use the name of their families of origin, but also wives took the surnames of their husbands affirming their slave marriages. And these were not simply names that were put on the roll and then forgotten, for the white session at Zion came to know and to refer to the slave members as people who belonged to black families and claimed their own names. Zion was thus one place in Charleston where black slaves publicly declared that they had a history, that they had an allegiance other than to their owners, and that at the deepest level of self-identity, where they named themselves, they used the names their own families had adopted through their years of bondage.[27]

There was, however, no question that this paternalism was, from the whites' perspective, a means of subordinating the blacks of the city. It allowed whites to accept without question the existing social structure while giving them at the same time an opportunity to strengthen the system through a paternal concern for the needs of the slave. But more than this, the paternalism of the Zion experiment allowed conscientious whites an opportunity to express their ideals of an organic community. Jones had taught in his catechism and Thornwell had emphasized in his sermon at the opening of the Anson Street Church the corporate nature of society in which each person has a particular place and function. Zion, as a community of believers who looked after one another's needs under the supervision and patronage of white masters, would provide a structure within the larger society in which this corporate ideal could be expressed. Zion would be an attempt to give some security to the black whose place in society was that of a "servant." It would be an attempt to provide the black slave with a sense of belonging, a feeling of loyalty, and an opportunity for mutual help.

The bitter irony of this attempt by whites to "work within the system" can be seen in the failure of the Zion experiment to provide any real security to the black slave. While the black membership of Zion grew to over five hundred by 1860 and up to fifteen hundred were attending the Sunday services, underneath there lay the radical insecurity of a slave. The radical nature of that insecurity and the fundamental weakness of a paternalistic ideal in a slave society can be clearly seen in the records of Zion and the other churches of Charleston.

The roll book of Zion had not only the name of the slave who had joined but also the name of the master or mistress. Beside many names there is eloquent testimony to the cruel story of the slaves: "Martha Foster, servant of John Otten, sold away from the city. Did not apply for a certificate; probably had not the opportunity to do so. She gave evidence of being a humble Christian." Time after time there appears the notation "sold away"—particularly toward the end of the 1850's as Charleston's economic prosperity declined and the activity of her slave markets increased. By 1859 it had become necessary for the white session of Zion to give Girardeau the unusual power to grant letters of dismissal to the blacks who were suddenly "sold away" from the city.[28]

It was in regard to the marriage of blacks that the consequences of this instability and the effects which it had upon the ideals of a corporate and stable society were most clearly revealed. The State gave no legal recognition to the marriage of slaves. Many of the Charleston churches, however, insisted on the sanctity of such marriages. The church records show the tension.

There was Martha who had been excommunicated from the First Baptist Church for adultery. She appeared before the Committee on Coloured Members and declared her guilt, professing "penitence for the same." She was, however, still living with the same man. Her husband, she said, had given her a release from all obligations to him as "he had been sent away without any hope of returning to the city." Her reason for not marrying the man with whom she was presently living was an objection on the part of her mistress. In view of all the circumstances of the case, Martha believed that the life she was leading was a virtuous one and that she should be received back into the church. The committee, however, recommended that she should ask her mistress once again for permission to marry as she "could not be restored while remaining in her present unlawful state of life."[29]

There was Perry Peak. He was a member of Zion Church who had left his wife in Alabama when his master had brought him to Charleston. Could he marry again? Or Dolly Fraiser? Her mother had joined the Second Church over thirty years ago and young Dolly had grown up hearing Smyth preach and reciting Jones' catechism. Now she had married without the permission of her master. What action was the Zion session to take? She was pregnant, but unmarried. She would have married, only the "proposed husband" could not get permission from his master. Similar cases were abundant in the records of other churches. Years later a former slave would remember the break-up of a black Charleston family:

> One mornin' a couple married an' de next mornin' de boss sell de wife. De gal ma got out in de street an' cursed de white woman fur all she could find.

The mother, who ended up in the Charleston workhouse, had cried in the streets that "Dat damn pale-faced bastard sell my daughter who jus' married las' night."[30]

The Protestant Episcopal Convention of the Diocese of South Carolina appointed in 1858 a special committee to report on the "Duty of Clergymen in Relation to the Marriage of Slaves." The committee, headed by C. G. Memminger, published its report in which it sought to clarify under what circumstances a clergyman could "unite slaves in marriage." For wise and sufficient reasons, declared the report, the state

> has committed to the master a discretionary power to dispose of his slaves. The mode of exercising that power is left to the conscience of the master. If that master should disregard the commands of God, and be led by caprice or self-interest to separate those who are lawfully joined together in marriage, he incurs all the consequences of his act, and must answer for it to the Final Judge. But the innocent parties who have been separated, stand

upon a different footing, and are objects of sympathy and not of censure. They are deprived by an external authority, of all the benefits of the marriage relation; they can no longer fulfill its obligations, and if the separation be continued and final, they are virtually dead to each other. Under such circumstances the marriage no longer subsists but in name.

Here was essentially the same position as other churches had adopted in a less formal manner and used for a number of years.[31]

This statement reveals in summary both the paternalism of southern whites and the radical flaws that undercut its ideals. The responsibility of the master in regard to his slave's marriage reflects the paternalistic order which southern whites sought to develop. There is throughout all of this a dream of obtaining a religious and social wholeness for the community that Thornwell had advocated in his sermon and that the white religious leaders of Charleston had sought to put into practice. All people, they had said, are united together before God, however unequal they may be in this world. Yet at the same time, and perhaps at a deeper level, there is revealed here in these church records not only a southern paternalism with a corporate view of society, but a southern individualism, a modern Protestant individualism, which views each person as ultimately standing alone. The emphasis was on the *personal* relationship between master and slave rather than on the structures of society. Neither paternalistic order nor the institution of marriage was as important as the relationship between master and slave. The master alone, according to these records, was to act as the final judge of the slave's marriage and was to decide what was an avoidable or unavoidable separation of husband and wife. A careful study of church records reveals no incident of a slave owner ever being disciplined by any of the Charleston churches for destroying a slave marriage. Slave owners were admonished, suspended, and excommunicated for many things, but not for selling a husband or wife, a parent or child away from loved ones. Presumably in the eyes of white church officers there were always "mitigating circumstances." At any rate, the decision was "left to the conscience of the master" who had to answer only to "the Final Judge." The position and the security of the slave were thus seen to depend upon the will of the master and not upon the discipline of the church or some stable rules that govern society.

Beyond even this individualism, however, lay the fact that ultimately these whites, like their slaves, were part of an economic system: whites were owners of black men, women, and children. As owners they and their slaves were subject to all the forces of an economic system that regarded blacks not as children but as valuable assets to be managed in an economical manner.

This meant that a truly paternalistic society, beyond its obvious injustice and oppression, was an impossible dream for southern whites. The paternalism which the Charleston churches sought was never fully realized within the structures of a slave society. However intimately slaves may have been a part of the community, they were still slaves. The family—the basic unit and fundamental model of paternalism—was in fact never secure for the slave.

Conclusion

I

White preachers and black slaves in Liberty County, Georgia, and Charleston, South Carolina, were joined together in a complex web of relationships that were often ambiguous and frequently filled with deep pathos and profound ironies. Both had their lives shaped and warped by slavery, with the white preachers helping to forge the chains and the black slaves suffering the raw wounds of the shackles. Yet both from their radically different positions were able on occasion and in their own ways to transcend the degradation they suffered because of slavery. For the white preachers this meant discovering, beneath the rhetoric of slavery that they had done so much to create, the humanity of black slaves and therefore something of their own humanity. For the black slaves this meant discovering beneath and perhaps through their suffering their identity as a people—Afro-Americans, slaves in Egypt seeking the Promised Land. White preachers were, unfortunately, unable to transform their insights into more than calls for paternalistic reforms within the system of slavery. Black slaves, however, were able to transform their insights not only into a sense of personal dignity but also into a black church that was a center of their community giving unity and common purpose to their people.

From the moment Charles Jones came back to Liberty County as an eager young missionary to "the heathen in our midst," and, throughout the story of the Charleston churches, it was clear that white preachers were seeking to work within the system of slavery to instill a submissive spirit into the hearts of black people. Their preaching, their teaching, their pastoral labors, and the way they organized the structures of the church—all were intended to make blacks both dependent and obedient servants. This was obvious not only to the preachers but to the slaves as well. It would be a mistake, however, to think that these white preachers saw this as their primary goal, as if they somehow felt called to give their lives to making good servants, for that would be a misunderstanding of the motivation behind their labors. It would be an easy and in many ways deserved judgement upon those who did so much to support an incredibly cruel system, but it would be missing the bitter irony of their lives.

Charles Jones and the white ministers of Charleston saw their primary responsibility to be the conversion of lost sinners and the nurture of the faithful. This was true of their efforts in regard to both blacks and whites. They believed that there was a heaven and a hell, an eternal reward for the faithful and an eternal damnation for the unfaithful. They believed that the eternal was more important than the historical, the spiritual than the material. This was fundamental for them. It shaped their perspectives on all of life and informed their ministerial efforts. Jones would spend 150 pages of his catechism making an evangelical presentation of the faith and only 4 pages presenting the "duties of masters and servants." But he did have a section on "duties," and he and his ministerial friends believed that morals and manners were important, very important. They were indications, external signs, of an internal faith; they were marks of a disciple, part of the discipline of the Christian faith.

Because they were convinced of the brevity of this earthly life and its relative insignificance beside the eternal, and because they emphasized the duties of both masters and slaves, these white preachers thought of themselves as moderates. Strange as it seems in light of their support of slavery, they considered themselves to be standing between extremes in regard to the black slaves of the South. The abolistionists they considered anarchists; those Southerners who would treat slaves as mere chattel property they regarded as radicals and as great a danger to the South as abolitionists. Both they judged to be infidels who ignored the clear dictates of the Bible. Even James Henley Thornwell, called the "Calhoun of the Southern Church," would declare in the debate over the opening of the Anson Street Church that

> as the Bible condemns the unruly, the seditious, the radical, the abolitionist and the agrarian, so it is equally hostile to *the infidel, the carnal* and the anti-christian spirit which sets itself against furnishing ample religious instruction to the slave.[1]

It was from this "moderate" position that white preachers sought to minister to the blacks of Liberty County and Charleston. They labored to present the gospel which they feverently believed would save the souls of blacks and whites from damnation; they spoke frequently and freely of the responsibilities of owners to provide good food, adequate housing, and security for the slave family; and they sought to provide within the structures of the church a place where blacks could not only worship but have some space they could call their own, where they could have their own leaders and provide each other with mutual support and encouragement.

There was, however, much painful irony hidden along the paths of these white preachers. In their belief that they could be moderates, that they could stand between extremes on the question of slavery, they did not see that such a system ultimately would demand that they make a choice on one side or the other. They thought that they could find a humane middle way and did not perceive how they themselves were slipping more and more into extremes. Charles Jones had written as a young man that slavery was "a violation of all the laws of God and man at once. A complete annihilation of justice. An inhuman abuse of power, and an assumption of the responsibility of fixing the life and destiny of immortal beings, fearful in extreme." A number of the cosmopolitan ministers in Charleston had shared similar views as young men. Their understanding of themselves as moderates was perhaps based on the memory of these earlier perceptions as they sought to live and work in an increasingly defensive and isolated South. Yet they became staunch pro-slavery advocates, with some moving faster in southern currents and others slower, so that by 1861 men like Jones, Bachman, and Smyth would be praying openly for a "slave holding confederacy," where slavery would be a "blessing to ourselves, to our slaves, and to the world at large."[2]

Even greater than their illusions about moderation, however, was the belief that they could be paternalistic and humane in the midst of slavery. Their calls for reforms—for better housing, kinder treatment, and respect for slave marriages—blinded them to the fundamental inhumanity of the system. Even when these appeals emerged out of a genuine concern for the welfare of black slaves and were not simply a means of strengthening the system, they were nevertheless hollow. They were hollow because they had little power in the face of a powerful economic and social system and because they could not challenge its fundamental injustice: the ownership of people as valuable property.

These white preachers were a bitter generation. Sophisticated, educated in northern and European universities, well-traveled, they knew the increasing isolation of the South and its growing condemnation. And they knew with the coming of the Civil War what Jones had feared as a young man—the overthrow of slavery with a "tenfold vengeance." Yet they loved the South, its land and its people. Some of them cared deeply (one must say it though their caring was narrow and patronizing) for the black slaves who lived and labored around them. They sought to do their duty in this land, to fulfill their responsibilities to their "servants," and they gave much of their lives and energies in their behalf. They were, nevertheless, an obsessed generation, for they also gave themselves to the defense of an impossible cause and poured out their powers in an attempt to justify human bondage. If, however, the vain pretensions of these white preachers who tried to follow a middle way, and the sorrows of their slaves, thus keep them from being Tragic Figures, their labors can evoke from all whose heart knows its own bitterness, the knowing smile of good intentions gone astray. That knowing smile was, in an amazing manner, the response of many of the black slaves who knew the kindness of white preachers and yet were not deceived by their pretensions.

II

The black slaves of Liberty County and Charleston received the attention of these white preachers in a manner that revealed not only the degradation to which they were subjected as slaves, but also their peculiar strength as a people in bondage struggling toward freedom.

Their degradation could be seen most clearly in their treatment by cruel or indifferent owners, but it also emerged in their acceptance of the kind and condescending attention of humane whites who set out to do what they considered to be "just and equal." When black slaves, surrounded by all the power and cruelty of slavery, accepted the dependance and submission taught by white preachers, something of their human dignity was demanded. That it was something given—even as a lesser evil— was part of the profound tragedy that blacks suffered under slavery. Those blacks who did become "Sambos" or "Uncle Toms" owed much of their humiliation to the white preachers who sought to instill in their souls the duty of submission.

The amazing fact, however, is that many black slaves did not internalize the submission taught by white preachers, and that they used the church and its message as one of their major sources for resistance. Blacks heard not only from their own hearts and experience, not only from their own leaders, but from white preachers that they were children of God. Such a message, if not revolutionary, was liberating in the sense that it reminded slaves of their dignity and humanity in the face of all the forces that sought to deny them. The fact that these same white preachers, who did so much to support slavery, also helped to speak this liberating word of affirmation explains in some measure the ambiguity with which blacks regarded white preachers. Thus at the end of the Civil War, the black members of Zion would continue to come to hear Girardeau preach while at the same time they struggled against his old attitudes. This struggle would finally lead to Zion's becoming a strong black church with its own black session and black preacher. Yet over a hundred years later, when a new church building was erected, the black congregation would remember this white preacher and include in one of its stained glass windows the picture of Girardeau.[3]

Of much greater importance for slaves as a source of self-worth and resistance was the emergence of the black church *within* the white controlled churches. This was particularly true in Charleston where the urban setting provided greater opportunity for the black church to develop a strong institutional expression. This development would reflect the primary difference between the urban and plantation black churches. The difference would be a matter of degree, but it would be a significant degree. In Liberty County, the black church was weaker and had fewer opportunities to organize in ways that were helpful to scattered plantation slaves. Here the church was more of a "secret institution," the faith and hope of individuals bound tightly together in slavery, but only loosely connected in the church under the black watchmen. In Charleston, however, a strong institutional expression of the black church existed well before the Civil War.

No acknowledged independent black church was allowed in Charleston after the destruction of the AME Church in 1821.

Blacks were able to use the paternalism of whites, however, to find the space within the churches of Charleston to establish a black church. It was, to paraphrase E. Franklin Frazier, "a church within a church." Here it was a "secret institution," not so much in the sense that it met in secret—though there was no doubt some of that—but rather in the sense that it was hidden within the structures of the white church. The pretentions of whites generally blinded them to the existence of such a church. There would be occasions when whites would acknowledge its presence, as when Thornwell noted that the black leaders and not the white preachers were the real "wire pullers" among the black church members; but generally whites failed to perceive the extent to which blacks had organized their own institution within the white churches. Blacks had no such problem and used every opportunity to strengthen the black church as the primary institution for a developing Afro-American culture where leaders were nurtured, education provided, a sense of solidarity and discipline developed, and mutual help supplied.[4]

These well-known characteristics of the black church after the Civil War were clearly present and developing through the years of slavery in the midst of the white controlled churches of Charleston and, to a lesser extent, Liberty County. Leadership in the black community found its focus and opportunity in this church within a church. The watchmen or class leaders were men of ability and piety who used the approval of whites and blacks to develop their own authority. They taught, they "exhorted," they exercised discipline, they comforted the sorrowing, they buried the dead and brought relief to the needy. In all of this they were not only preparing the way for the strong black preachers who would openly emerge as leaders in the black community following the Civil War but they were themselves black preachers, the leaders within the slave community. Just as the black church was hidden within the structures of the white controlled church, these black preachers were hidden beneath the rubrics of paternalism. Their titles were carefully chosen, their duties narrowly defined, their activities closely watched, but they were able to forge a place for themselves that would only be openly acknowledged after emancipation. If they could not now be called a preacher or "Reverend," they could make the title "watchman" or "leader" indicate a position of authority and respect among blacks; if they could not preach, they could exhort and care little for the careful distinctions that whites made between the two. If final decisions on important matters of church discipline were in the hands of the whites, they could settle lesser matters, carefully choose and shape to their own purposes the presentations before the whites, and use the discipline of the church to bring some order and cohension to a black community constantly threatened by the disorder and chaos of slavery. In all of this, they were showing that they did not have to be passive; they were proving that, even in the face of a powerful and cruel system, men and women could resist the degradations of slavery, assert their dignity, and seek to build a community of faith and hope.

One of the primary responsibilities of the leaders was to teach. After the closing in 1835 of the few black schools that had existed in Charleston, the church became the central place for any formal education of blacks. It had, no doubt, always been the most important location in terms of the numbers it reached—the schools operated by Daniel Payne, Thomas Bonneau, and the Minors' Moralist Society were all primarily intended for free blacks. In the churches, however, the blacks, both free and slave, were all divided into classes with their own leaders. In the three Methodist churches alone there were more than seventy such classes meeting all over the city, from Goose Creek to Old Bethel, with an average of forty pupils for each class. All total, there were by 1860 more than 150 such classes meeting at least once a week throughout the city. While these classes focused on religious instruction, and while whites sought to keep some supervision over them, there can be no question that they represented the most important agency that blacks had for providing themselves with an education. The instruction was oral, but many of the leaders could read and write—they often had to give written

reports to white church officers—and no doubt they found opportunity in their lessons and exhorting to teach of a broader
world than Charleston and slavery. Moreover, it was an opportunity to interpret, of necessity in a circumspect and careful manner, their experience as a people.

That black men and women were able to build within the bonds
of slavery these organs of nurture and resistance which would
later emerge so powerfully in their struggle toward freedom and
dignity is a tribute not only to their resourcefulness but also to
their faith that was forged in the hot fires of suffering and oppression.

III

While black slaves were thus able to use to their own advantage
the paternalism of whites, this did not prevent them from seeing
through the pretensions of their oppressors. Blacks knew only
too well that, whatever opportunities for resistance might be
found in the kind but condescending attitudes of whites, that
whatever individual benevolence might be exhibited by a master,
all were overshadowed and swallowed up by the power of a cruel
system—even when the owner was a sympathetic and humane
white preacher.

In 1857 Charles Jones decided that it was necessary to sell a
young slave named Jane. She had been a troublemaker, as had
several members of her family, and when she ran away to Savannah it had been the final straw. Jones had never before sold a
slave, but decided that he could no longer keep her because of
the trouble she had caused and because, as his son said, her "tales
of Savannah and of high life in the city would probably not have
the most beneficial effect upon her compeers." Yet Jones had
been preaching for over twenty-five years that slave families were
not to be divided because of "dishonest character or conduct,"
or disruption of "the peace or arrangement" on the plantation.

In light of these convictions, he decided to sell Jane's whole family together. "Our determination to sell the whole family was based," he wrote his wife, "on these considerations: (1.) An indisposition to separate parents and child, no matter how evil their conduct had been in the premises. (2.) The unreliable character of the family, the trouble the mother has always given, and the moral certainty that, whenever occasions offer, the same rebellious conduct will appear again. (3.) And in case of the sale of the present incorrigible runaway apart from her family, although they have sent her away never to return, the effect upon them in all probability will not be for the better. (4.) And lastly, a change of investment would be more desirable than otherwise."

These were the considerations of a white preacher who gave most of his life and energies to the black slaves of Liberty County and the South. He was a kind master, a man who possessed, in the words of Robert Manson Myers, a "radiant Christian character, aptly described by his son-in-law as 'one of the noblest men God ever made.' " Yet there appears in his rationale for selling Jane and her family not only a final revealing statement about a "change of investment" being desirable, but a blindness that hid from him the terror of slavery and his involvement in its inhumanity even when he was attempting to be kind and to give to his "servants that which is just and equal."[5]

The irony was that Jones thought he could, as a humane master, keep the family together and thereby perserve his own innocence in the midst of slavery. He could do neither. Economic considerations finally forced him to keep several of Janes' older sisters, and the new owner did not keep his promise in regard to the remaining slave family. Through this sale, Jones separated Jane and her family from Liberty County which had been their home for years and cut them off from a wide range of family and friends.[6] Jane's parents, Phoebe and Cash, suffered many things in the anguish of leaving home and friends, but they suffered none of Jones' illusions. In a remarkably rare letter from New Orleans back to a Mr. Delions in Liberty County, they told their story:

NEW ORLEANS MARCH 17TH 1857

Pleas tell my daugher Clairissa and Nancy a heap how a doo for me
Pheaby and Cash and Cashes son James we left Savanah the first of
Jany we are now in New Orleans. Please tell them that their sister Jane
died the first of Feby we did not know what was the matter with her
some of the doctors said that she had the Plurisly and some thought
that she had Consumption. although we were sold for spite I hope that
it is for our own good but we cannot be doing any better than we are
doing very well. Mr Delions will please tell Cato that what [food] we
have got to t[hrow] away now it would be anough to furnish you
Plantation for one season Mr Delions will please answer this Letter for
Clairssa and Let me know all that has hapened since i left. Please tell
them that the Children were all sick with the measles but they are well
now. Clairssa your affectionate mother and Father sends a heap of
Love to you and your Husband and my Grand Children Phebea. Mag
& Cloe. John. Judy. Sue. My Aunt Aufy sinena and Minton and Little
Plaska. Charles Nega. Fillis and all of their Children. Cash. Prime.
Laffatte. Rick Tonia [send their love] to you all. Give our Love to
Cashes Brother Porter and his wife Patience. Victoria gives her Love
to her Cousin Beck and Miley
    I have no more to say untill i get a home. I remain your affectionate
Mother and Father

Pheobia and Cash

P.S. Please give my love to Judys Husband Plaska and also Cashs love.
Pheobe and Cash send a great deal of Howdie for Mr Adam Dunumn
and Mr Samuel Braton.[7]

However humane Jones may have thought himself, with whatever
good intentions he may have approached the "problem" of Jane
and her family, this black family knew the reality of what Jones
had declared twenty-five years earlier as a young man—that the
"assumption of the responsibility of fixing the life and destiny of
immortal beings" was "fearful in the extreme."
    If the experience and insights of Phoebe and Cash reveal
clearly the pretensions of Jones and other white preachers, another remarkable letter reveals even more clearly the suffering of
black slaves—even when their masters were kind. Abream was the
husband of Jones' slave Dinah. His master for some unknown
reason decided that he must be sold. Abream was, wrote Jones'
son Charles Jr., "in a very distressed frame of mind, not knowing

who will be his purchaser, and with the probability staring him in the face of his being carried far away from his wife and children, to whom he appears to be sincerely attached. It is a hard case," noted the younger Jones, "and I would in a moment purchase and send him to the Island were such a thing practical. As it is, we can only regret the sad fact of his being thus parted without the means of preventing the separation."[8] Charles Jr. and his father wanted to act in a responsible manner as Christian gentlemen who were genuinely concerned about the welfare of slaves. What they failed to see, however, was their own involvement in this tragedy and how slavery shaped and warped their own lives. They were the owners of Dinah Jones. They assumed responsibility for her life and destiny. They were as much a part of this tragedy and the tragedy of the South as Abream Scriven's owner. Their kind paternalism did not do what they had hoped. It did not perserve their innocence.

SAVANNAH SEPT THE 19TH 1858

Dianh Jones
My Dear wife I take the pleasure of writing you these few [lines] with much regret to inform you that I am Sold to a man by the name of Peterson atreader and Stays in new orleans. I am here yet But I expect to go before long but when I get there I will write and let you know where I am. My Dear I want to Send you Some things but I donot know who to Send them By but I will thry to get them to you and my children. Give my love to my father & mother and tell them good Bye for me. and if we Shall not meet in this world I hope to meet in heaven. My Dear wife for you and my Children my pen cannot Express the griffe I feel to be parted from you all
I remain your truly husband until Death

Abream Scriven[9]

Abream Scriven never again met his wife in this world. When he made inquiries about her following the Civil War, he found that she had died.

Jones and his son, being genuinely kind and humane men, would have purchased Abream Scriven and saved him and his family their grief—if it had been practical. . . .

Epilogue

I

Charles Colcock Jones retired from his missionary labors in January, 1848. "It has been a long, laborious work," he told the planters of Liberty County, "little seen even by those among whom it has been performed, having its cares and anxieties, and many and some great discouragements." But, he went on,

> I have experienced many comforts and rewards also. The confidence, the affection, and the gratitude of the people themselves, have been a continual refreshment to my soul. I have loved their salvation and sought it, and the evident benefit accruing to them temporally and spiritually, which has attended the humble work . . . and the conviction that I was in the path of duty, and that God would in due time bring the people out of darkness into light of the Gospel all over the land and save them, has been my stay and my support.[1]

Convinced that he was following the path of duty and that he had received the gratitude of the blacks, he had labored until his health had failed. His doctors warned him that he could no

longer stand the strains of his work—particularly the exposure
that came with riding about in the night to the various plantations
to preach and visit among the slave cabins and to talk with the
slave masters. He had accepted, therefore, a professorship at the
theological seminary in Columbia and he hoped that his work
there, instead of removing him "from the coloured field," would
open to him "in several respects a more wide and permanent
influence of it."[2] He would remain in Columbia for two years
before moving on to Philadelphia to head the Presbyterian Board
of Domestic Missions giving special emphasis to the religious
instruction of slaves. But Philadelphia would be no better for his
health than the damp night air of Liberty County, and in 1853,
he would return to Montevideo. Until his death in 1863, he would
remain a semi-invalid, preaching to slaves when well, writing his
posthumously published history of the church, and watching with
satisfaction the daily life of his plantations and the growing prosperity of his children.

Jones' last public utterance came on December 10, 1861, at the
first General Assembly of the Presbyterian Church in the Confederate States of America. Here he spoke once again to slaveholders about the duties divine providence had placed upon them.
His address was a reiteration of what he had been saying to
Southerners for thirty years, a final plea for the work that had
claimed his life, and an eloquent testimony to the power of the
South over the heart and imagination of its people. As the armies
of the North prepared to trample out the vineyards of wrath, and
the armies of the South prepared to take their stand in Dixie,
Jones dreamed once more of bringing the gospel to the slaves:

> Yes, my brethren, there is a blessing in the work. How often,
> returning home after preaching on the Sabbath-day, through
> crowds of worshippers—sometimes singing as they went down to
> their homes again; or returning from plantation meetings held in
> humble abodes, late in the star-light night, or in the soft moon-
> light, silvering over the forests on the roadside, wet with heavy
> dews, with scarcely a sound to break the silence, alone but not
> lonely—how often has there flowed up in the soul a deep, peaceful
> joy, that God enabled me to preach the Gospel to the poor.
> . . .[3]

For the blacks of Liberty County, there was little cause for such nostalgic musings. From 1848, when Jones retired from his missionary work, until the Civil War, their lives continued to be filled with their labors in the rice and cotton fields, with their struggles against sickness and death and the oppressions of slavery. "Your people all seem to be doing very well," wrote Cato, the black foreman at Montevideo, to Jones in Philadelphia. "They attend praise & go to church regularly whenever there is preaching in reach. We have had a good deel of Sickness among the children from worms, but no very ill cases. . . . We are this week working on the roads with our men. I have been for parts of two weeks on our marsh Stopping the big cut which I am Satisfied is now Secure & Raising the river dam all around which is a big job & will take up much time yet but you will be pleased with the way we are putting it up. . . . The marsh has astonished Every boddy that has seen it it is very fine cotton & Especially all the oldest Stocks from the first planting, we have now all the women picking cotton & from appearance will have no more time to do anything else. . . . The rice crop Looks fair all things considered. . . ."4

Cato had earlier reported to Jones the troubles he was having with Cash and Phoebe (it was a prelude to Jones' decision to sell them with their daughter Jane) and sought constantly to ingratiate himself with Jones: "I always feel satisfied," he wrote Jones, "that I have a good Shear of your Love and Confidance, but whenever I See you take the time & trouble, to write me your Servant a kind & I may say fatherly letter, it makes me feel more like crying with love & grattitude for So kind a master than any thing else, and always feel it in my heart to say, I will try and be a better Servant than ever. . . ." Jones had himself written to Cato: "We have been together a long time, and I have always had a great attachment to you and confidence in you: and you have always been a good and faithful man to me."5

But Jones had also written years before that whites "live and die in the midst of Negroes and know comparatively little of their real character." Blacks were, he said, "one thing before whites, and another before their own color." The correctness of this observation would be revealed with stunting clarity during and immediately after the Civil War as Cato and other Liberty County slaves deserted their former owners. Jones would not live to see the full extent of it, but the handwriting would be on the wall before his death. "A public meeting of the citizens was called on the 8th at Hinesville," wrote Jones to his son in 1862, "to adopt some measures for suppressing if possible the escape of our Negroes to the enemy on the coast. *Fifty-one* have already gone from this county. Your Uncle John has lost five. *Three* are said to have left from your Aunt Susan's and Cousin Laura's; one was captured, two not; and one of these was *Joefinny!* . . . None may be absolutely depended on. . . . Our people *as yet* are all at home, and *hope* they may continue faithful."[6]

That was the hope—that they would continue faithful, that they would act not simply out of obedience or fear, but out of respect, loyalty, and affection. And some did. Mom Kate and Mom Lucy would be faithful to the end of their days. Gilbert and Charles would be models of fidelity. But these were the exceptions, and the widowed Mary Jones was left to experience what Eugene Genovese has called "the terrible moment of truth." "I am throughly disgusted with the whole race," she wrote her daughter in 1865. "I could fill my sheet with details of dishonesty at Montevideo and Arcadia, but my heart sickens at the recital, and a prospect of dwelling with them. For the present it appears duty to do so." Years earlier duty had called a young Charles Jones to return home and take up the burden of a "neglected race"; now it called Mary Jones to remain in Liberty County among the ruins of a happier time and the devastations that followed Sherman's march to the sea. And the expectation was that because they had followed what they had understood to be their "path of duty," the blacks would be grateful. Yet Patience and Porter would prove "unfaithful," and Susan who had been the nursemaid to the Jones' grandchild "acted a faithless part as soon as she could," giving information to the Yankees. William and Kate who had been married in the Jones' parlor, served their marriage breakfast in the Jones' kitchen, and kept together through the efforts of Charles, Jr., left Montevideo not to return. And there were others, many others; but Cato, who had expressed such loyalty, love, and gratitude toward Jones, would prove the worst of all. He would stir up trouble at Montevideo before any of the others and would behave toward Mary Jones in an "insolent, indolent, and dishonest" manner.[7]

That was the bitter revelation—that the blacks of Liberty County had acted more out of obedience and fear than out of respect, loyalty, and affection. They had, on the whole, been obedient before emancipation, and some would even be faithful during the hard days after the war; but when the opportunity came, most would claim their freedom, they would show that their first obligation was not to their former owners but to themselves and their people. If kind owners like Charles and Mary Jones had done their duty—well, it had been their duty and gratitude was not in order. This did not mean, however, that the former slaves turned their backs completely on the past, that it was finished and forgotten, but rather that they faced the future from a new stance. And no where was that clearer than in regard to the church.

It would be primarily to the church that they would turn in the years ahead as a focal point in their lives which gave cohesion and strength to their people. They would organize churches at the old preaching stations where Jones had labored so long and where they themselves had worshipped and found strength and nurture during the years of slavery—at Midway and Sunbury, Newport and Pleasant Grove. Now, however, these were black churches, not preaching stations for slaves. If the blacks of Liberty County proved unfaithful to their old owners, they would struggle to be faithful to a pilgrimage they had begun in slavery and to the One who had been their rock in a weary land. That, however, is another story and it waits to be told in another book.[8]

II

On May 13, 1865, Daniel Payne sailed into Charleston Harbor on the federal ship Arago. His arrival was thirty years to the day after he had left the city in exile following the close of his school for blacks and twenty years to the day after Charles Colcock Jones, John Bachman, William Capers, and a host of other distinguished whites had gathered on Chalmers Street to discuss "the religious instruction of the Negro." Now at the war's end, Payne returned to his native city as the most influential bishop in the African Methodist Episcopal Church.

As his ship rounded Morris Island and entered the harbor, Payne could see, as Jones had seen years earlier, the outline of Charleston. At this first sight of his native city he was struck by "indescribable feelings," with pleasure and sad emotion "rapidly interchanging." The proud old "Capital of the South" lay in ruins. White Point Garden, at the tip of the peninsula, was covered with grotesque earthwork defenses. Fort Sumter was a broken rubble. Huge holes and mounds of earth blocked lower Meeting Street as part of the unfinished inner ring of city defenses. "Destruction," wrote Payne of his survey of the city, "marked every square through which we passed." Even worse than the destruction of the war had been the ravages of a fire in 1861. Beginning almost at the edge of the Cooper River, it had cut a wide path across the peninsula until it had burned itself out near the edge of the Ashley. Payne found only burned walls at the old Cumberland Church where he had once worshipped and a gutted frame at the Circular Congregational Church where his friend Benjamin Palmer, Sr., had been pastor. It all showed, Payne was sure, "the hot indignation of the God who, when he stretches out his arm against the oppressor, never draws it back till every fetter is broken and every slave is free."[9]

Payne found a number of old friends he still knew and recognized after his separation of thirty years. There were the Holloways who had continued to maintain their harness shop at 39

Beaufain Street and to play an active role in the Methodist churches of the city. Samuel Weston was still alive, although he and his family had suffered greatly because of the fire and the war. He had been Payne's class leader at the Cumberland Church and when Payne had been forced to leave the city, it was Weston who had given him a suit to travel in. Now, thirty years later, Bishop Payne would ordain his old class leader as a minister in the African Methodist Episcopal Church.[10]

Payne spent his first Sunday in Charleston attending an early morning prayer meeting with the black members of the Circular Church, preaching in the Zion Presbyterian Church and later that evening at Old Bethel. It was a day that revealed much about the future direction of the black churches in Charleston and their relationship to white preachers and white congregations.

The black members at the Circular Church would continue a part of that congregation for two more years. In 1867 they would address a letter to the congregation asking to be regularly dismissed from the old church to begin their own separate congregation. The request was granted and the Plymouth Congregational Church was formed with the Reverend F. L. Cordoza as the pastor. He was a native of Charleston who had been in his youth a member of the Second Presbyterian Church. His father, a wealthy Jewish economist, had sent him to Edinburg where he had eventually studied theology. In the years ahead, he would play an important role in the reconstruction government of the state.[11]

The pattern at the Circular Church was followed by many of the blacks in the other Charleston churches. Those who were members of the First Baptist Church separated in a friendly manner from the white members of the congregation and formed what came to be known as the Morris Street Baptist Church. Jacob Legare, who had been their leader for over fifteen years at the First Baptist Church, became their pastor at Morris Street. At the Second Presbyterian, the blacks withdrew to form a congregation on Glebe Street, while those across the street at the Citadel Square Baptist Church organized the Calvary Baptist. At

Bethel Methodist, which held so many memories for both blacks and whites, the biracial character of the congregation was maintained until 1878 when the old church building was rolled from its place beside a newer building to a site on Calhoun Street and the black members organized Old Bethel Methodist Church. It was a pattern that was repeated all over the city—black congregations emerged from within the old white-dominated churches to form their own strong and vigorous churches. Like the black members of the Circular Church and Bethel Methodist, many did not withdraw immediately at the close of the war, but stayed and struggled for several years in an attempt to work out, as free men and women, a new relationship to their old churches. When they did withdraw, they did so as clearly defined congregations with their own particular histories and leaders, and not simply as individuals going their separate ways.

It was not by accident that Payne preached on his first Sunday morning in the Zion Presbyterian Church. Zion had become identified in the years immediately before the war as a center of the black community in Charleston. It would remain so during the years immediately after the war. In many ways, however, the old paternalistic ethos would remain strong at Zion. Girardeau would return from a Union prison camp to begin preaching once again to large numbers of blacks. Time and again he would refuse to accept calls to influential white churches throughout the South because of his strong sense of duty to the blacks of the city. If, however, this old paternalism died hard, it did die. Girardeau would be the only member— despite his eloquent appeals—of the Southern Presbyterian General Assembly to vote against the formation of a separate black denomination. He was convinced blacks and whites ought to remain together after the old pattern. But the old pattern was now repugnant to both blacks and whites, and Girardeau accepted a call to Columbia Theological Seminary, where Charles Jones and James Henley Thornwell had taught and where his old predecessor at Anson Street, John Adger, was now a professor. In 1878, Zion would call its first black minister, William C. Smith, and join the Northern Presbyterian Church.[13]

Of much greater importance than Zion would be the work of the AME Church that Payne organized in Charleston. Meeting once again in the Zion Church, Payne formed on May 15, 1865, the South Carolina Annual Conference. This AME conference would provide in the years to come outstanding religious and educational leadership to the blacks of the state. It was, however, the first congregation that the conference organized that touched most deeply the hearts and memories of the Charleston blacks— they named it Emmanuel, "God with us," after the old Emmanuel Church that had been closed at the time of the Denmark Vesey insurrection. It was a reorganization, they insisted, of the old church that Morris Brown had served; it was a declaration that they had a history as a people, that they were not simply slaves who had been shaped by their masters, but Afro-Americans who remembered their past and who honored those who had struggled for the freedom of their people. Emmanuel would immediately become and would remain for the next hundred years the strongest and most influential AME church in the South. With such a history and such a future, it would be a clear expression of an unfolding Afro-American culture that had its roots deep in the experience of its people, and its sharpest institutional focus in the life of the church.[14]

On the same day that Emmanuel was reorganized, Payne visited the newly established schools for the black children of the city. Over three thousand were being taught by teachers from the North under the control, wrote Payne, of "so radical an abolitionist as James Redpath," with the "protection of United States black troops." Remembering, no doubt, his own school closed thirty years earlier, Payne's emotions overwhelmed him. With the colonel of the Massachusetts regiment at his right and Major Alexander Augusta on his left, Payne shed tears of "gratitude, thanksgiving, and love to that God who had wrought such a marvelous change in the condition of a helpless race." And he remembered a prayer offered in his behalf when he was forced to leave the city. Written in a note to him by Mary Palmer, daughter of Benjamin Palmer, pastor of the Circular Church, it had declared "O Lord of hosts, blessed is the man that trusteth in thee."[15]

NOTES

Notes to the Introduction

1. Frederick Law Olmsted, *The Cotton Kingdom* (New York: Mason Brothers, 1862) II, p. 215.

Notes to Chapter 1

1. James Stacy, *History of the Midway Congregational Church, Liberty County, Georgia*, rev. ed. (Newnan, Ga.: S. W. Murray, 1903), pp. 1–20; E. Merton Coulter, *Georgia, A Short History*, rev. and enlarged ed. (Chapel Hill: University of North Carolina Press, 1947), p. 96.

2. Stacy, *History of Midway*, pp. 27–34; Robert Manson Myers, ed., *The Children of Pride: A True Story of Georgia and the Civil War* (New Haven: Yale University Press, 1972), pp. 8–9.

3. On the names "Medway" and "Midway," see Stacy, *History of Midway*, pp. 23–27.

4. Myers, *Children of Pride*, p. 8.

5. The slave population remained stable during the thirty years preceding the Civil War. See Charles C. Jones, *Annual Report of the Missionary to the Negroes, in Liberty County, (Ga.) Presented to the Association, November 1833* (Charleston: Ob-

server Office Press, 1834), p. 5; Charles C. Jones, *Seventh Annual Report of the Association for Religious Instruction of the Negroes in Liberty County, Ga. Together with the Address to the Association by the President, The Rev. Josiah Spry Law. The Constitution of the Association. And the Population of the County for 1840* (Savannah: Thomas Purse, Printer, 1842); and the United States Census of 1850 and 1860.

6. Stacy, *History of Midway*, pp. 58–59; R. Q. Mallard, *Plantation Life Before Emancipation* (Richmond, Va.: Whittet and Shepperson, 1892), pp. 14–19.

7. See Work Projects Administration, *Drums and Shadows: Survival Studies among the Georgia Coastal Negroes* (Athens: University of Georgia Press, 1940), *passim.*

8. *Ibid.*, pp. 116, 66, 67, 159, 161, 162, 164, 166; Lydia Parrish, *Slave Songs of the Georgia Sea Islands* (1942; reprint ed., Hatboro, Penn.: Folklore Associates, Inc., 1965), pp. 45–47.

9. Charles C. Jones, *Tenth Annual Report of the Association for the Religious Instruction of the Negroes in Liberty County, Georgia* (Savannah: Office of P. G. Thomas, 1845), pp. 13–14.

10. Cf. Kenneth M. Stampp, *The Peculiar Institution: Slavery in the Ante-Bellum South* (New York: Random House, Inc., A Vintage Book, 1956), p. 185.

11. Major John Jones, Charles' grandfather, came to the Midway community from Charleston, S. C., building his home in the costal village of Sunbury. He was killed on October 9, 1779, at the Battle of Savannah fighting the British. "Genealogy," Charles Colcock Jones Collection, Tulane University, New Orleans, La. (This collection is hereafter cited as JCTU.)

12. Mallard, *Plantation Life*, pp. 91–100; R. Q. Mallard, *Montevideo-Maybank: Some Memoirs of A Southern Christian Household in the Olden Time; or, The Family Life of the Rev. Charles Colcock Jones, D. D., of Liberty County, Ga.* (Richmond: Presbyterian Committee of Publication, 1898); Myers, *Children of Pride*, pp. 11–31. (This monumental collection of the letters of the Jones family begins in 1854 after Jones had ended his active labors as the missionary for the Liberty County Association for the Religious Instruction of the Negroes. This present study focuses on an earlier period than that covered by *Children of Pride.*) See also Robert Manson Myers, *A Georgian at Princeton* (New York: Harcourt Brace Jovanovich, 1976) for the period 1850–1852, and Eduard N. Loring, "Charles C. Jones: Missionary to Plantation Slaves, 1831–1847" (Ph.D. diss., Vanderbilt University, 1976).

13. Charles C. Jones to Elizabeth J. Maxwell, October 4, 1825, JCTU; Charles Jones to Mary Jones, September 8, 1829, JCTU.

14. See Sydney E. Ahlstrom, *A Religious History of the American People* (New Haven and London: Yale University Press, 1972), pp. 394, 396, 415–28.

15. Charles Jones to Elizabeth J. Maxwell, September 6, 1828, JCTU.

16. Charles Jones to Mary Jones, July 22, 1829, and September 8, 1829, JCTU.

17. Charles Jones to Mary Jones, July 9, 1829, JCTU.

18. Charles Jones to Mary Jones, May 18, 1830, JCTU.

19. John Miller Wells, *Southern Presbyterian Worthier,* (Richmond, Va.: Presbyterian Committee of Publication, 1936), pp. 50–76.

20. Charles Jones to Mary Jones, December 8, 1829, February 3, 1830, and May 18, 1830, JCTU.

21. Charles Jones to Mary Jones, February 3, 1830, JCTU.

22. Mallard, *Montevideo-Maybank;* Myers, *Children of Pride,* p. 18.

23. Myers, *Children of Pride,* p. 19.

24. *Ibid.,* pp. 1301–1313.

25. Catoe Jones to Charles Jones, September 3, 1852, JCTU; also found in Robert S. Starobin, ed., *Blacks in Bondage: Letters of American Slaves* (New York: New Viewpoints, 1974), pp. 47–50.

26. Frederick Douglass, *Life and Times of Frederick Douglass* (New York: Collier, 1962), p. 97.

27. Charles C. Jones, *Thirteenth Annual Report of the Association for the Religious Instruction of the Negroes, in Liberty County, Georgia* (Savannah: Edward J. Purse, Printer, 1848), p. 59.

Notes to Chapter 2

1. Charles Jones to Mary Jones, September 18, 1830, JCTU.

2. Myers, *Children of Pride,* "Who's Who," pp. 1449–1738; Jones, *First Annual Report,* pp. 2–5; Charles Jones to Mary Jones, Sept. 18, 1830, JCTU.

3. Charles C. Jones, *The Religious Instruction of the Negroes, A Sermon, Delivered before Associations of Planters In Liberty and McIntosh Counties, Georgia,* 4th ed. (Princeton: O'Hart and Connolly, 1832), pp. 6–7 (hereafter cited as Jones, *RIN. A Sermon*).

4. *RIN. A Sermon,* pp. 12–13.

5. Charles Jones to Elizabeth J. Maxwell, September 6, 1828; Charles Jones to Mary Jones, February 3, 1830; Charles Jones to Mary Jones, May 8, 1830; Charles Jones to Mary Jones, May 18, 1830; Charles Jones to Mary Jones, June 5, 1830; Charles Jones to Mary Jones, June 24, 1830; Charles Jones to Mary Jones, July 23, 1830; Charles Jones to Mary Jones, August 25, 1830; all found in the JCTU.

6. *RIN. A Sermon,* pp. 18–19.

7. *Ibid.,* pp. 25–28.

8. *Ibid.,* pp. 29–30. See Also Charles C. Jones, *The Religious Instruction of the Negroes, In the United States* (Savannah: Thomas Purse, 1842), pp. 208–210 (hereafter cited as RINUS).

9. Jones, *RIN. A Sermon,* pp. 30–32.

10. Jones, *Tenth Annual Report,* p. 14. Charles C. Jones, *Seventh Annual Report, passim.*

11. Jones, *Thirteenth Annual Report,* p. 61; Jones, *Tenth Annual Report,* p. 15–18; *Minutes of the Synod of South Carolina and Georgia, December 3, 1831,* p. 294. Charles Jones to Elizabeth Maxwell, September 19, 1831; Charles Jones to Mary Jones, December 3, 1831; Charles Jones to Mary Jones, December 6, 1831; all letters in JCTU.

12. Charles C. Jones, *Eleventh Annual Report of the Association for the Religious Instruction of the Negroes, in Liberty County* (Savannah: Office of P. G. Thomas, 1846), p. 15; Charles C. Jones, *Twelfth Annual Report of the Association for the Religious Instruction of the Negroes, in Liberty County, Georgia* (Savannah: Edward C. Councell, 1847), pp. 11–12; Stacy, *History of Midway,* p. 169.

13. (Charles C. Jones), *Report of the Committee to Whom Was Referred the Subject of the Religious Instruction of the Colored Population, of the Synod of South-Carolina and Georgia. At Its Late Session in Columbia, South-Carolina, December 5th–9th, 1833 (Charleston: Observer Office Press, 1834), p. 6.*

14. See Charles C. Jones, *Suggestions of the Religious Instruction of the Negroes in the Southern States; together with an Appendix Containing Forms of Church Registers, Form of A Constitution, And Plans of Different Denominations of Christians* (Philadelphia: Presbyterian Board of Publication, 1847), p. 38 (hereafter cited as Jones, SRINSS); and Jones, RINUS, p. 274.

15. Stacy, *History of Midway*, p. 170; Jones, *First Annual Report*, p. 6.

16. Jones, *Tenth Annual Report*, p. 18; Jones, *First Annual Report*, p. 6; Stacy, *History of Midway*, pp. 76, 112.

17. Stacy, *History of Midway*, pp. 166–67, 174; Jones, *Tenth Annual Report*, p. 10; Jones, *First Annual Report*, p. 6; Jones, *Seventh Annual Report*, p. 3; Jones, *Eleventh Annual Report*, p. 6.

18. Jones, *First Annual Report*, p. 8; Jones, *Fifth Annual Report of the Association for the Religious Instruction of the Negroes in Liberty County, Georgia. January, 1840* (Charleston: Observer Office Press, 1840), p. 10; Jones, *Tenth Annual Report*, pp. 10–16.

19. Jones, *Fifth Annual Report*, p. 19; Jones, *Tenth Annual Report*, pp. 8, 32; *Seventh Annual Report*, pp. 3–4; *Minutes of the Presbytery of Georgia, January 1, 1842*, 2:57–58.

20. Stacy, *History of Midway*, pp. 164–68, 189–93; *Minutes of the Session, Midway Congregational Church*, May 20, 1837.

21. Stacy, *History of Midway*, p. 168.

22. Stacy, *History of Midway*, pp. 189–93; *Minutes of the Session, Midway Congregational Church*, May 20, 1837; Jones, *Tenth Annual Report*, p. 25; Jones, *Twelfth Annual Report*, p. 7.

Notes to Chapter 3

1. Jones, *Seventh Annual Report*, p. 4; Jones, *Thirteenth Annual Report*, pp. 10, 33; Jones, *Tenth Annual Report*, p. 32.

2. Jones, *Seventh Annual Report*, p. 4; Jones, *Tenth Annual Report*, p. 32.

3. Stacy, *History of Midway Church*, pp. 58–61, 261–81.

4. Jones, *RINUS*, p. 256.

5. *Ibid.*, p. 252.

6. Jones, *SRINSS*, p. 14.

7. Jones, *RINUS*, p. 261, pp. 110–11.

8. J. Leighton Wilson, *Western Africa: Its History, Condition, and Prospects* (New York: Harper & Brothers, 1856); see *Charleston Observer*, 1834–1845, *passim*, for reports from Africa by Wilson.

9. Jones, *RINUS*, p. 261.

10. Jones, *SRINSS*, p. 14; Jones, *RINUS*, p. 256.

11. Jones, *RINUS*, pp. 255, 262; cf. Jones, *SRINSS*, p. 15 and Jones, *Tenth Annual Report*, pp. 41–42.

12. Jones, *RINUS*, p. 259; cf. Jones, SRINSS, p. 15.

13. Jones, "The Salvation of the Soul," sermon written August 4, 1832; Jones, "Lay Not Up For Yourselves Treasures Upon the Earth," sermon written May 28, 1841; Jones, "When a Wicked Man Dieth, His Expectation Shall Perish," sermon written August 11, 1838. These and all of the following unpublished sermons by Jones are in the Jones Collection, Tulane University.

14. Jones, *Third Annual Report*, p. 13; Jones, "Eliezer, Gen. 24: 1–67," sermon written March 15, 1834, JCTU.

15. Jones, "Character of Gehazi, Servant of Elisha, the *Man of God*," sermon written July 12, 1833, JCTU.

16. Jones, *Tenth Annual Report*, p. 24; cf. Eugene Genovese, *Roll, Jordan, Roll: The World The Slaves Made* (New York: Pantheon Books, 1972), pp. 202–206.

17. Jones, *Tenth Annual Report*, p. 24; Jones, *Third Annual Report*, p. 14.

18. Cf. WPA, *Drums and Shadows, passim.*

19. Jones, "Simon the Sorcerer," sermon written March 28, 1834; Jones, "The Person and Character: Occupation and Influence of the Wicked One: And the Duty of Christians in respect thereto," sermon written June 13, 1841, JCTU.

20. Jones, "Our Lord Cleanses the Temple," sermon written March 13, 1841. Typical of other sermon titles in the Tulane Collection are "The Temptation of Christ," Nahum 1:3, "The Lord Is Slow To Anger, And Great In Power, And Will Not At All Acquit the Wicked," "The Marriage State and Honor Of It," and "The Life and Death of Jeboram, the Son Of Jehoshaphit. A discourse to Youth."

21. Mallard, *Plantation Life*, pp. 88–89.

22. Jones, *Seventh Annual Report*, p. 8; Jones, *Tenth Annual Report*, p. 22.

23. Jones, *RINUS*, p. 265.

24. Parrish, *Slave Songs*, pp. 56–57.

25. *Ibid.*, pp. 71–72.

26. *Ibid.*, p. 161.

27. "The Negro Spirituals," *The Atlantic Monthly*, XIX (June 1867), p. 685.

28. "Slave Songs on a Mission," *Southern Christian Advocate* [Charleston, S.C.], VII (December 29, 1843), p. 114.

29. *Ibid.*

30. Charles C. Jones, *A Catechism of Scripture, Doctrine and Practice: For Families and Sabbath Schools, Designed also for the Oral Instruction of Colored Persons*, 3rd ed. (Savannah: T. Purse and Co., and New York: Leavitt, Trow & Co., 1845), p. 11 (hereafter cited as *CSD & P*).

31. Jones, *RINUS*, pp. 265–66.

32. Jones, *SRINSS*, p. 25.

33. Jones, *First Annual Report*, pp. 9–10; Jones, *Third Annual Report*, p. 4.

34. Jones, *Tenth Annual Report*, p. 42; Jones, *RINUS*, p. 251; Jones, *CSD & P*, p. 80.

35. Cf. Donald G. Mathews, *Slavery and Methodism: A Chapter in American Morality, 1780–1845* (Princeton: Princeton University Press, 1965), p. 77.

36. Jones, *RINUS*, p. 264; *Tenth Annual Report*, pp. 21–22; Jones, *Catechism for Colored Persons*, p. iii; Jones, *Third Annual Report*, p. 5.

37. Jones, *CSD & P*, p. 69.

38. Jones, *CSD & P*, p. 2.

39. Jones, *Catechism for Colored Persons*, p. 95. Jones did say that God's knowing and seeing all was helpful to those who love Him, for God was with the slaves to bless them and help them in trouble or sickness. There was thus a tension between the threat and blessing of God's activity. See *ibid.*, pp. 6–7.

40. Jones, *CSD & P*, p. 131; see also *RINUS*, p. 211.

41. Jones, *CSD & P*, pp. 127–29.

42. *Ibid.*, pp. 129–31.

43. See Jones, *Tenth Annual Report*, pp. 9–10, and Stacy, *Midway Congregational Church*, p. 173. For the role of older men in the slave community, see Herbert G. Gutman, *The Black Family in Slavery and Freedom, 1750-1925* (New York: Pantheon Books, 1976), p. 219.

44. *Minutes of the Session, Midway Congregational Church*, 1833, 1838.

45. Jones, *Tenth Annual Report*, pp. 27–28.

46. Jones, *Minutes of Watchmen's Meeting for Midway Church, Instituted March 8th, 1840, By the Consent and Order of the Church*, JCTU, pp. 1–2.

47. *Minutes of the Session, Midway Congregational Church*, 1833–1837; Jones, *Minutes of Watchmen*, pp. 7–12; see also Jones, *Tenth Annual Report*, pp. 21, 31; Jones, *Eleventh Annual Report*, pp. 11–13.

48. Jones, *RINUS*, p. 217.

49. See Gutman, *The Black Family in Slavery and Freedom*, pp. 219–22; Genovese, *Roll, Jordan, Roll*, pp. 607–608, 658–60.

50. Jones, *Seventh Annual Report*, p. 3; Jones, *Tenth Annual Report*, p. 41; see Jones, *RINUS*, p. 99, where he estimates from 150 to 500 attending.

51. Jones, *Seventh Annual Report*, p. 5; Jones, *Eleventh Annual Report*, pp. 16–18; Jones, *Twelfth Annual Report*, p. 13.

52. Jones, *Tenth Annual Report*, p. 39; Jones, *Eighth Annual Report*, p. 17; *Minutes of the Session, Midway Congregational Church*, 1833–1847; Jones, *Eighth Annual Report*, p. 12.

53. Jones, *Eighth Annual Report*, p. 19; *Minutes of the Session, Midway Congregational Church*, 1833–1847; for the tenacity of the African heritage, see WPA, *Drums and Shadows, passim*.

54. Jones, *RINUS*, p. 215.

Notes to Chapter 4

1. Jones, *RINUS*, p. 267; Mallard, *Plantation Life*, pp. 16–17, 104, 166; cf. Myers, *A Georgian at Princeton*, p. 303; the black slaves of Thomas Mallard are identified

through *Minutes of the Session, Midway Congregational Church,* 1833–1847, and Mallard, *ibid.,* pp. 51, 54–61.

2. Jones, *Tenth Annual Report,* p. 23; Jones, *Third Annual Report,* p. 4.

3. Jones, *First Annual Report,* p. 7; Jones, *RINUS,* p. 267; Mallard, *Plantation Life,* pp. 61, 92.

4. Jones, *First Annual Report,* pp. 7–8; Jones, *Eighth Annual Report,* p. 4; Jones, *Tenth Annual Report,* p. 41.

5. Jones, *Eleventh Annual Report,* p. 20; Jones, *RINUS,* p. 243; Jones, *Tenth Annual Report,* p. 38; Mallard, *Plantation Life,* p. 104.

6. Jones, *Eleventh Annual Report,* p. 10.

7. See Jones, *First Annual Report,* p. 8; Jones, *Tenth Annual Report,* p. 23; Jones, *Thirteenth Annual Report,* p. 10; Jones, *RINUS,* pp. 17, 268; and Mallard, *Plantation Life,* p. 105.

8. Mallard, *Plantation Life,* pp. 29–31, 17–19; Jones, *SRINSS,* p. 17.

9. Jones, *Third Annual Report,* p. 11; Jones, *Tenth Annual Report,* pp. 16–17.

10. Charles Jones to Mary Jones, November 4, 1835; and Charles Jones to Mary Jones, November 6, 1835, JCTU.

11. Commenting upon the importance of Jones' *The Religious Instruction of the Negroes in the United States,* John R. Bodo has written ". . . the facts he marshalled came to be used far and wide in countering abolitionist attacks on the Southern churches and their clergy." In John R. Bodo, *The Protestant Clergy and Public Issues, 1812–1848* (Princeton: Princeton University Press, 1954), p. 146.

12. Charles C. Jones, *Address to the Senior Class in the Theological Seminary of South Carolina and Georgia, on the Evening of the Anniversary. Columbia, July 10th, 1837,* (Savannah: Thomas Purse & Co., 1837), p. 10; cf. Jones, *Third Annual Report,* p. 6; and Jones, *RINUS,* pp. 186–87.

13. Jones, *RINUS,* pp. 208–10; cf. Jones, *Tenth Annual Report,* p. 40.

14. Jones, *Seventh Annual Report,* p. 10; Jones, *RINUS,* p. 208.

15. Jones, *RINUS,* p. 275; Jones, *SRINSS,* pp. 33–35; Jones, *Seventh Annual Report,* pp. 7–8.

16. Jones, *Thirteenth Annual Report,* p. 21; see also Jones, *SRINSS,* pp. 35–36; Jones, *CSD & P,* p. 104; Jones, *RINUS,* p. 162.

17. Jones, *Eleventh Annual Report,* pp. 17–18; Jones, *RINUS,* pp. 138–39.

18. Jones, *First Annual Report,* pp. 13–14.

19. Jones, *RINUS,* pp. 119, 241.

20. Jones, *Twelfth Annual Report,* pp. 18–21; Jones, *Third Annual Report,* p. 6.

21. Jones, *RINUS,* p. 16; Jones, *Thirteenth Annual Report,* p. 13–16; Jones, *RINUS,* p. 240; Mallard, *Plantation Life,* pp. 29–30; for warnings of southern agricultural

periodicals about the importance of good housing, see Kenneth Stampp, *The Peculiar Institution* (New York: Alfred A. Knopf, 1956), p. 293.

22. Jones, *RINUS*, pp. 115–16; Mallard, *Plantation Life*, p. 32.

23. Jones, *SRINSS*, p. 35; Mallard, *Plantation Life*, pp. 31–32; see also Jones, *RINUS*, p. 241.

24. Jones, *RINUS*, p. 209; see also Jones, *CSD & P*, p. 128; Jones, *SRINSS*, p. 35; Jones, *RINUS*, p. 242.

25. Catoe Jones to Charles Jones, March 3, 1851, JCTU; also found in *Blacks in Bondage*, p. 54.

26. Mallard, *Plantation Life*, p. 34.

27. Jones, *CSD & P*, p. 128.

28. Jones, *Second Annual Report*, p. 9; Jones, *SRINSS*, p. 35; Jones, *RINUS*, p. 241.

29. Mallard, *Plantation Life*, pp. 23–37; Myers, *Children of Pride*, pp. 185–86, 643–46, 1154.

30. Jones, *RINUS*, p. 132; Charles C. Jones, *The History of the Church of God during the Period of Revelation*, Part I: "The Church during the Old Testament Dispensation" (New York: Charles Scribner & Co., 1867), pp. 21–22.

31. Jones, *RINUS*, p. 133.

32. Jones, *Thirteenth Annual Report*, pp. 17–18.

33. Jones, *Thirteenth Annual Report*, pp. 17; Mallard, *Plantation Life*, p. 51; *Minutes of the Session, Midway Congregational Church*, 1833–1847.

34. Jones, *Thirteenth Annual Report*, p. 16.

35. Jones, *ibid.*

36. *Minutes of the Session, Midway Congregational Church*, May 18, 1839; August 24, 1839; on the question of the interpretation of such statistics, see Herbert G. Gutman, *Slavery and the Numbers Games* (Urbana: Univ. of Illinois Press, 1975).

37. Mallard, *Plantation Life*, pp. 48; Myers, *Children of Pride*, pp. 243–271, *passim;* but, see pp. 168–70.

38. *Minutes of the Session, Midway Congregational Church*, October 21, 1835; February 19, 1848; August 17, 1850; Mallard, *Plantation Life*, pp. 52–53.

39. Myers, *Children of Pride*, see "Index: The Slaves" for page listings for these and other family connections.

40. Jones, *Seventh Annual Report*, pp. 4–5; Charles Jones, "The Marriage State. Nature and Honor of it," sermon written January 8, 1841, JCTU; Jones, *Catechism for Colored Persons*, p. 80.

41. Jones, *CSD & P*, p. 110; Jones, *Tenth Annual Report*, p. 27; see also Jones, *RINUS*, pp. 232–33; Jones, *SRINSS*, p. 23. For marriage ceremonies among slaves see also pp. 134, 155.

42. Myers, *Children of Pride*, pp. 178, 186, 643–46.

43. *Ibid.*, p. 1154.

44. *Ibid.*, pp. 996–98, 1001, 1008, 1011, 1016, 1020, 1026, 1028, 1310.

Notes to Chapter 5

1. Richard C. Wade, *Slavery in the Cities: The South 1820–1860* (New York: Oxford University Press paperback, 1967), pp. 10–12.

2. *Ibid.*

3. Cf. W.J. Cash, *The Mind of the South* (New York: Vintage Books, Random House, 1941), pp. 5–8, 61–81.

4. See Avery O. Craven, *Civil War in the Making, 1851–1860* (Baton Rouge: Louisiana State University, 1959).

5. See Frederic Bancroft, *Slave Trading in the Old South* (New York: Frederick Ungar Publishing Co., 1959), pp. 165–96.

6. "Autobiography of the Rev. Paul Trapier," (Publication of the Dalcho Historical Society of the Diocese of South Carolina, no. 17); Thomas Smyth, *Autobiographical Notes, Letters and Reflections,* ed. Louisa Cheves Stoney (Charleston, S. C.: Walker, Evans & Cogswell Company, 1914), pp. 215–16, 242–43.

7. Edward Guerrant Lilly, *Beyond the Burning Bush: First (Scots) Presbyterian Church, Charleston, S.C.* (Charleston, S. C.: Garnier & Company, 1971), pp. 44–45.

8. George Howe, *History of the Presbyterian Church in South Carolina* (Columbia, S. C.: W. J. Duffie, 1883), II, pp. 191–212.

9. Thomas Leonard Williams, "The Methodist Mission to the Slaves" (Ph.D. diss., Yale University, 1943), pp. 32–57.

10. Peter Guilday, *The Life and Times of Bishop England, First Bishop of Charleston* (New York: The American Press, 1927), II, *passim;* Madeleine H. Rice, *American Catholic Opinion in the Slavery Controversy* (New York: Columbia University Press, 1944), pp. 56–70.

11. Ahlstrom, *A Religious History,* p. 578.

12. Smyth, *Autobiographical Notes,* pp. 226–45.

13. Henry Allen Tupper, *Two Centuries of the First Baptist Church of South Carolina* (Baltimore: R. H. Woodward & Company, 1889).

14. Raymond Morris Bost, *The Reverend John Bachman and the Development of Southern Lutheranism* (Ph. D. diss., Yale University, 1963; Ann Arbor, Mich.: University Microfilms).

15. For a readily available comparison of census statistics, see Wade, *Slavery in the Cities,* pp. 325–30.

16. For discussions on the free black experience in general and in Charleston in particular, see Ira Berlin, *Slaves Without Masters: The Free Negro in the Antebellum South* (New York: Random House, Pantheon Books, 1974); Marina Wikramanayake, *A World in Shadow: The Free Black in Antebellum South Carolina* (Columbia, S. C.: University of South Carolina Press, 1973); E. Horace Fitchett, "The Traditions of the Free Negro in Charleston, South Carolina," *Journal of Negro History,* XXV (1940), 139–51; *idem,* "The Origins and Growth of the Free Negro Population of Charleston, South Carolina," *Journal of Negro History,* XXVI (1941), 421–37; *idem,* "The Status of the Free Negro in Charleston, South Carolina, and

His Descendants in Modern Society," *Journal of Negro History,* XXXII (1947), 430–51.

17. Quoted in Wade, *Slavery in the Cities,* pp. 251–52.

18. *Charleston Mercury,* May 5, 1845; *Charleston Courier,* May 9, 13, 1845.

19. John B. Adger, *My Life and Times* (Richmond, Va.: The Presbyterian Committee of Publication, 1899), pp. 34–40; Smyth, *Autobiographical Notes,* pp. 61–65, 73–76.

20. Smyth, *Autobiographical Notes,* pp. 115–16, 383.

21. Cf. Wade, *Slavery in the Cities,* pp. 55–59.

22. Adger, *My Life and Times,* p. 167.

23. Wade, *Slavery in the Cities,* pp. 21–23; Smyth, *Autobiographical Notes,* pp. 325, 393, 625, 347.

24. Smyth, *Autobiographical Notes,* p. 325.

25. Wade, *Slavery in the Cities,* pp. 38–54.

26. *Charleston Courier,* September 20, 1845; Smyth, *Autobiographical Notes,* p. 108.

27. Wade, *Slavery in the Cities,* pp. 180–208.

Notes to Chapter 6

1. *Proceedings of the Meeting in Charleston, S. C. May 13–15, 1845, on the Religious Instruction of the Negroes, together with the Report of the Committee, and the Address to the Public* (Charleston: B. Jenkins, 1845), p. 15 (hereafter cited as *Proceedings*).

2. See Laura White, *Robert Barnwell Rhett* (New York: Century, 1931).

3. Catherine H. Birney, *The Grimké Sisters: Sara and Angelina Grimké, The First American Women Advocates of Abolition and Woman's Rights* (Westport, Conn.: Greenwood Press, 1969).

4. *Charleston Mercury,* May 2, 10, 14, 1845.

5. *Proceedings,* pp. 15–16.

6. *Ibid.,* pp. 16–17.

7. *Charleston Mercury,* May 12, 1845.

8. *Proceedings,* p. 18.

9. *Ibid.,* pp. 6–8.

10. *Ibid.,* p. 9.

11. *Ibid.*

12. *Ibid.,* pp. 7–8.

13. *Ibid.,* p. 8.

14. *Ibid.,* pp. 10–11.

15. Bost, *The Reverend John Bachman,* p. 430.

16. See William Sumner Jenkins, *Pro-Slavery Thought in the Old South* (Chapel Hill: The University of North Carolina Press, 1935), pp. 242–84; William Stanton, *The Leopard's Spots: Scientific Attitudes Toward Race in America 1815–1859* (Chicago: University of Chicago Press, 1960).

17. See, for example, Samuel George Morton, *Crania Aegyptiaca* (Philadelphia: J. Dobson, 1844), pp. 22–29.

18. Quoted in Jenkins, *Pro-Slavery Thought*, p. 250.

19. Quoted with disgust by Thomas Smyth in Thomas Smyth, *Unity of the Human Races* (New York: Putnam, 1850), p. 351.

20. Smyth, *Autobiographical Notes*, p. 246; Bost, *The Reverend John Bachman*, pp. 433–34.

21. John Bachman, *The Doctrine of the Unity of the Human Race Examined on the Principles of Science* (Charleston: C. Canning, 1850), p. 119.

22. Smyth, *Unity of the Human Races*, p. 74.

23. *Ibid.*, p. 45.

24. Stanton, *The Leopard's Spots*, p. 173; Smyth, *The Unity of the Human Races*, p. 325.

25. Smyth, *The Unity of the Human Races*, pp. 330, 333–34, 344; Bachman, *The Doctrine of the Unity of the Human Race*, p. 8.

Notes to Chapter 7

1. *Minutes of the Annual Conference of the Methodist Episcopal Church in South Carolina*, 1856.

2. Mood, *Methodism in Charleston*, pp. 184–85, 87.

3. *Minutes of the Charleston Baptist Association*, 1845.

4. *Journal of the Proceedings of the Protestant Episcopal Church in the Diocese of South Carolina, 1825–1860; Minutes of the Synod of the Presbyterian Church in South Carolina, 1845–1860;* Bost, *The Reverend John Bachman*, pp. 125, 404.

5. *St. Mary's Vestry, 1832–1855*, ms. (Archives, St. Mary's Church, Charleston); *Baptismal Records of Saint Paul's Catholic Church, Charleston, S. C.*, ms. (Diocesan Archives, Charleston); Guilday, *The Life and Times of Bishop England*, II, pp. 156, 297; Rice, *American Catholic Opinion in the Slavery Controversy*, pp. 69–70.

6. *St. Mary's Vestry, 1832–1855; Record of the Colored Members in the Methodist Church, Charleston, S. C., 1821–1880*, ms. (Archives, Trinity Methodist Church, Charleston); *Roll Book, Second Presbyterian Church, Charleston*, ms. (Historical Foundation of the Presbyterian and Reformed Churches, Montreat, N. C.); *Register of the Coloured Members of the Third Presbyterian Church*, ms., *ibid.; Communicant Roll Books of Colored Members of Zion Presbyterian Church*, ms., *ibid.; Church Register, St. John's Lutheran Church, 1852–1922*, ms. (Archives, St. John's Lutheran Church, Charleston); *Minutes, St. John's Lutheran Church, 1837–1845*, ms., *ibid.; The Private Register of the Rev. Paul Trapier* [St. Michael's Episcopal Church] (Publication of the Dalcho Historical Society of the Diocese of South Carolina, No. 7); *Minutes of the Board of Deacons, First Baptist Church, Charleston, S.C., 1847–1870*, ms. (Archives, First Baptist Church, Charleston).

7. *Proceedings of the Meeting in Charleston, S. C., May 13–15, 1845*, p. 38 f.; Bost, *The Reverend John Bachman*, p. 389.

8. Smyth, *Autobiographical Notes*, pp. 393–94; *Minutes of the Session of the Second Presbyterian Church, Charleston, S. C., 1832–1860*, ms. (Historical Foundation of the

Presbyterian and Reformed Churches, Montreat, N.C.,). For the history of black preachers, see Charles V. Hamilton, *The Black Preachers in America* (New York: William Morrow and Company, 1972), and Genovese, *Roll, Jordan, Roll,* pp. 255–79.

9. *Minutes of the Session of the Second Presbyterian Church, Charleston, S. C., 1832–1860,* September, 1850; *Record Book, Circular Congregational Church, 1824–1861,* ms. (Archives, Circular Congregation Church, Charleston) July, 1848; Bost, *The Reverend John Bachman,* p. 389, *Minutes of the Board of Deacons, First Baptist Church,* September 8, 1851.

10. Susan Markey Fickling, "Slave-Conversion in South Carolina, 1830–1860," *Bulletin of the University of South Carolina,* No. 146 (Columbia: University of South Carolina Press, 1924), p. 18; for black leaders giving written reports to white church officers, there was, for example, the requirement at the Circular Congregational Church that black leaders give written reports on the reformation of those blacks who had been suspended and were applying to be restored to the fellowship of the church, *Record Book, Circular Congregational Church, 1828–1861,* June 24, 1844.

11. Bishop Daniel Alexander Payne, *Recollections of Seventy Years* (New York: Arno Press and The New York Times, 1968), pp. 14–40; Bost, *The Reverend John Bachman,* pp. 393–400.

12. Fickling, "Slave-Conversion in South Carolina," p. 18; George P. Rawick, ed., *The American Slave: A Composite Autobiography,* vol. 3, South Carolina Narratives (Westport, Conn.: Greenwood Publishing Company, 1972), p. 167.

13. Mood, *Methodism in Charleston,* p. 188; *Minutes of the Session, Second Presbyterian Church,* March 17, 1845; *Communicant Roll Book of Colored Members of Zion Presbyterian Church,* 1855.

14. *Record Book, Circular Congregational Church,* February 18, 1856; *Minutes of the Board of Deacons, First Baptist Church,* February 11, 1850; *Cash Book and Financial Records of Cathedral Parish and the Diocese* [Roman Catholic] ms. (Diocesian Archives, Charleston); *Minutes of Cumberland Church Benevolent Society, Charleston, S. C.,* ms. (Archives, Trinity Methodist Church); *Minutes of the Session, Second Presbyterian Church,* December, 1848. For the later development of poor funds in black churches into black owned insurance companies, see James B. Browning, "The Beginnings of Insurance Enterprise Among Negroes," *Journal of Negro History,* XXII (1937).

15. *Record Book, Circular Congregational Church; Minutes of the Session, Second Presbyterian Church; Minutes of the Board of Deacons, First Baptist Church;* Bost, *The Reverend John Bachman,* pp. 389–90; *Record of the Colored Members in the Methodist Church, Charleston, S.C.*

16. *Record Book, Circular Congregational Church,* 1828–1861.

17. *Record of the Colored Members in the Methodist Church, Charleston, S.C.*

18. Smyth, *Autobiographical Notes,* pp. 205, 393–94; Bost, *The Reverend John Bachman,* pp. 390–403.

19. Mood, *Methodism in Charleston*, pp. 130–33; John Lofton, *Insurrection in South Carolina: The Turbulent World of Denmark Vesey* (Yellow Springs, Ohio: The Antioch Press, 1964), pp. 92–94; Robert S. Starobin, ed., *Denmark Vesey: The Slave Conspiracy of 1822* (Englewood Cliffs, N. J.: Prentice-Hall, 1970), pp. 1–9. Daniel A. Payne, *History of the African Methodist Episcopal Church* (New York: Arno Press and The New York Times, 1969), pp. 13–30.

20. Lofton, *Insurrection in South Carolina*, pp. 93–94.

21. *Record of the Colored Members in the Methodist Church, Charleston, S.C.* This record book lists sixty-eight classes formed in 1821 with fifty-two leaders and the names of 2,887 class members. Not one among the Charleston AME leaders mentioned by Payne is included.

22. Starobin, *Denmark Vesey*, pp. 8–9.

23. Payne, *History of the African Methodist Episcopal Church*, pp. 19–45.

24. *Charleston Courier*, July 17, 1847.

25. *Minutes, St. John's Lutheran Church, Charleston, S.C. 1830–1845*, ms. (Archives, St. John's Lutheran Church, Charleston), August 10, 1831; August 30, 1831; Bost, *The Reverend John Bachman*, pp. 388–89.

26. Mood, *Methodism in Charleston*, pp. 145–49; *An Exposition of the Causes Which Led to the Session from the Methodist Episcopal Church in Charleston, South Carolina* (Charleston: E. J. Brunt, 1834). For a discussion of this division as a "minor but symbolic episode of Evangelical history," see Mathews, *Religion in the Old South*, pp. 205–207.

27. *Sermons of Charleston Ministers* (Collection in the Smyth Library, Columbia Theological Seminary, Decatur, Ga.).

28. Smyth, *Autobiographical Notes*, p. 198; Henry Mitchell, *Black Preaching* (Philadelphia and New York: J. B. Lippincott Company, 1970), pp. 80–82.

29. Mood, *Methodism in Charleston*, p. 132; Smyth, *Autobiographical Notes*, p. 198.

30. *Sermons of Charleston Ministers; Minutes of the Annual Conference of the Methodist Episcopal Church in South Carolina*, 1845, p. 19.

31. Smyth, *Autobiographical Notes*, pp. 146, 684.

32. Bost, *The Reverend John Bachman*, pp. 126, 387.

33. *Records of St. Mary's Roman Catholic Church* (Diocesian Archives, Charleston); "The Private Register of the Reverend Paul Trapier," *Publication of the Dalcho Historical Society of the Diocese of South Carolina*, February 11, 1848.

34. *Minutes of the Board of Deacons, First Baptist Church*, May 5, 1848.

35. Jones, *CSD & P*, p. 151.

36. Lilly, *Beyond the Burning Bush: First (Scots) Presbyterian Church*, pp. 14–15. Similar services were held at the Second Presbyterian Church as early as 1814; *Minutes of the Session, Second Presbyterian Church*, 1814.

37. *Ibid.*

38. *Record of Marriages Performed by Rev. Edward Phillips, Employed as the Missionary to the Charleston Protestant Episcopal Domestic Missionary Society and Subsequently the Minister of St. Steven's Chapel, 1822–1860*, ms. (South Carolina Historical Society);

Minutes of the Session, Zion Presbyterian Church, October 25, 1859; see pp. 156–58 for the attempts of the churches to develop guidelines for the marriage of slaves.

39. *Minutes of the Board of Deacons, First Baptist Church,* July 11, 1847; January, 1848.

40. "The Private Register of the Reverend Paul Trapier," October 9, 1834. There is a question about the use of the phrase, "whom God hath joined together, let no man put asunder." Cf. Jones, *Thirteenth Annual Report,* p. 16, and Genovese, *Roll, Jordan, Roll,* pp. 480–81. I have used it here because of the formal setting for so many of the Charleston weddings and because of the position of the Charleston churches against the separation of husband and wife; see pp. 156–58. It was probably rarely used outside Charleston and a few other urban settings.

41. Mood, *Methodism in Charleston,* p. 189.

42. *Rules and Regulations of the Brown Fellowship Society Established at Charleston, South Carolina, 1st November, 1790* (Charleston: J. B. Nixon, 1844); Fitchett, "The Origin and Growth of the Free Negro Population of Charleston, South Carolina," *Journal of Negro History,* XXVI (1941), 424.

43. *Public Proceeding Relating to Calvary Church and the Religious Instruction of Slaves* (Charleston: Miller and Browne, 1850), p. 25; *Minutes of Quarterly Conference; Meetings of Cumberland Church and Trinity Church, 1854 to 1891,* September, 1859.

44. *Private Register of the Reverend Paul Trapier;* Wade, *Slavery in the Cities,* pp. 169–70, 270.

45. Quoted in Wade, *Slavery in the Cities,* p. 170.

46. *Minutes of the Session, Second Presbyterian Church,* May, 1850.

47. Thomas Smyth, *An Order for Funeral Services* (Boston: S.N. Dickinson, 1843); Smyth, *Autobiographical Notes,* p. 200; Wade, *Slavery in the Cities,* pp. 169–70. The charge for the hearse was $2.00 (*Minutes of the Session, Second Presbyterian Church,* May, 1850).

Notes to Chapter 8

1. Adger, *My Life and Times,* p. 137.

2. *Ibid.,* pp. 78, 137. In a letter to the session of the Second Church, Adger wrote "that you never can as a Church, do anything adequate to their necessities, so long as you and they are expected to worship in one building, and yet you suffer the white portion of your church to occupy the Minister and the Session morning, noon, and night." *Minutes of the Session, Second Presbyterian Church,* January, 1848.

3. James H. Thornwell, "Religious Instruction of the Black Population," *Southern Presbyterian Review,* I (December, 1847), 108.

4. Adger, *My Life and Times,* pp. 133–35.

5. Thomas Smyth, "The Claims of the Free Church of Scotland," *Collected Works,* III, pp. ii–iii, 505–506; Smyth, *Autobiographical Notes,* p. 240.

6. *Liberator,* April 12, 1844; see also W. P. Garrison and F. J. Garrison, *William Lloyd Garrison* (New York: The Century Co., 1885–1889), III, pp. 150–51.

7. Frederick Douglass, *Life and Times of Frederick Douglass* (New York: Collier, 1962), pp. 251–52; Smyth, *Autobiographical Notes,* p. 367; *Liberator,* April 22, 26, May 17, July 12, 1844.

8. Smyth, *Autobiographical Notes,* pp. 365–78.

9. *Evangelical Alliance. Report of the Proceedings of the Conference* (London: Partridge and Oakey, 1847), pp. xcviii, 290–95, 304–309; 460–75; Adger, *My Life and Times,* p. 137; Smyth, *Autobiographical Notes,* pp. 359–62.

10. Adger, *My Life and Times,* pp. 164–65.

11. *Minutes of the Session, Second Presbyterian Church,* May, 1847; January, 1848.

12. Adger, *My Life and Times,* pp. 166–67.

13. *Charleston Mercury,* July 26, 1847; Howe, *Presbyterian Church in South Carolina,* vol. II, pp. 609–10.

14. *Charleston Mercury,* July 23, 1847.

15. Thornwell, "Religious Instruction of the Black Population," p. 101.

16. Adger, *My Life and Times,* pp. 164–65; *Charleston Mercury,* August 16, 1847; *Minutes of the Session, Second Presbyterian Church,* April, 1817. Vesey joined the Second Presbyterian Church in April 1817, with two other "people of colour": Marshall Groning and John Miller. The fact that they were baptised and Vesey was not indicates that he had already been baptised and very well may have been a member of another church. There is no other mention of Vesey in the Session minutes other than the notation of his death in the roll of members, and that notation was the same used for other deceased members. The history of the church roll was carefully reviewed in 1845 by John Adger's brother-in-law, Thomas Smyth, and his brother William Adger, and Vesey's membership acknowledged, *ibid.,* June, 1845.

17. Paul Trapier, *The Religious Instruction of the Black Population. The Gospel to be Given to Our Servants. A Sermon Preached in Several Protestant Episcopal Churches in Charleston on Sundays in July, 1847.* (Charleston: n.p., 1847); Trapier, "Autobiography," pp. 27–28; Robert F. Durden, "The Establishment of Calvary Church, Charleston, S.C." *Publication of the Dalcho Historical Society of the Diocese of South Carolina,* 1965, pp. 64–71.

18. *Public Proceedings Relating to Calvary Church, And the Religious Instruction of Slaves* (Charleston: Miller and Browne, 1850).

19. Adger, *My Life and Times,* p. 178; Myers, *A Georgian at Princeton,* p. 15.

20. James H. Thornwell, "Slavery and the Religious Instruction of the Colored Population," *Southern Presbyterian Review,* IV (July, 1850): 136–41.

21. Durden, "The Establishment of Calvary Church," pp. 70–71; Adger, *My Life and Times,* p. 174.

22. George A. Blackburn, ed., *The Life Work of John L. Girardeau, D.D., L.L.D., Late Professor in the Presbyterian Theological Seminary, Columbia, S. C.* (Columbia: The State Company, 1916), pp. 70–72.

23. Smyth, *Autobiographical Notes,* pp. 194–201; Blackburn, *The Life Work of John L. Girardeau,* pp. 81–84.

24. *Minutes of the Session, Zion Presbyterian Church.*

25. *Ibid.,* 1859; Smyth, *Autobiographical Notes,* pp. 199–200; Blackburn, *The Life Work of John L. Girardeau,* pp. 101–102. Throughout 1859 there were various attacks on Girardeau and Zion by Charleston whites. Complaints ranged from the dress of blacks at weddings and church services to the rumored subversive activi-

ties of the church. On October 26, 1859, the session addressed a letter to the Charleston papers defending the church's activities and affirming the white officers' support of slavery, *Minutes of the Session, Zion Presbyterian Church.*

26. *Minutes of the Session, Midway Congregational Church;* Myers, *Children of Pride,* 1842–1845; for the implications of surnames for slaves, see Gutman, *The Black Family in Slavery and Freedom,* pp. 230–56.

27. *Minutes of the Session, Second Presbyterian Church; Record of the Colored Members in the Methodist Church, Charleston, S. C.; Register of the Coloured Members of the Third Presbyterian Church; Record Book, Circular Congregational Church; Communicant Roll Book of Colored Members of Zion Presbyterian Church.*

28. *Communicant Roll Book of Colored Members of Zion Presbyterian Church.*

29. *Minutes of the Board of Deacons, First Baptist Church,* September 13, 1847; January 11, 1848.

30. *Minutes of the Session, Zion Presbyterian Church; Minutes of the Session, Second Presbyterian Church; Record Book, Circular Congregational Church; Minutes of the Board of Deacons, First Baptist Church; Record of the Colored Members in the Methodist Church, Charleston, S. C.;* Gutman, *The Black Family in Slavery and Freedom,* p. 148.

31. *Report of the Special Committee Appointed by the Protestant Episcopal Convention, at its Session in 1858, to Report on the Duty of Clergyman in Relation to the Marriage of Slaves* (Charleston: Walter, Evans & Co., 1859), pp. 1, 5–6. As early as 1825, the session of the Second Presbyterian Church had declared that a "coloured member whose wife has been parted from him being sold and transfered to a distance, can marry again." *Minutes of the Session, Second Presbyterian Church,* April 16, 1825. A more comprehensive ruling was made by the session in November, 1846. The Methodists, in 1859, issued the most detailed rules to be followed by any of the churches in Charleston. These included the course to be followed if a spouse, presumed to be "sent away" for ever, returned to the city: "If wife or husband sent off shall return, the church will not decide which shall be the husband or wife—the one sent off and returned or the one taken during his or her absence; but should any immorality be practised by either part, the delinquent shall be punished as the law of the church directs." *Minutes of Quarterly Conference Meetings of Cumberland Church and Trinity Church, 1854 to 1891,* ms. (Archives, Trinity Methodist Church, Charleston, S.C.); cf. also Bost, *The Reverend John Bachman,* p. 387.

Notes to Conclusion

1. Thornwell, "The Religious Instruction of the Black Population," pp. 107–108.

2. See above, pp. 00; cf. Smyth, *Autobiographical Notes,* pp. 78; *idem, A Soldier's Prayer Book* (1862); *Works,* VII, p. 725; Bost, *The Reverend John Bachman,* pp. 514–15.

3. Edward Guerrant Lilly, ed., *Historic Churches of Charleston* (Charleston: John Huguley Company, Inc. 1966), pp. 154–55; cf. Genovese, *Roll, Jordon, Roll,* pp. 202–209.

4. E. Franklin Frazier, *The Negro Church in America* (New York: Schocken Books, 1964), pp. 20–46.

5. Myers, *Children of Pride,* pp. 243, 255, 12.

6. *Ibid.,* pp. 240–71 *passim.*

7. Phoebia and Cash to Mr Delions, March 17, 1857, JCTU; also found in Starobin, *Blacks in Bondage,* pp. 57–58.

8. Myers, *Children of Pride,* p. 442.

9. Abream Scriven to Dinah Jones, September 19, 1858, JCTU; also found in *Blacks in Bondage,* p. 58; Myers, *Children of Pride,* p. 1147.

Notes to Epilogue

1. Jones, *Thirteenth Annual Report,* pp. 62–63.

2. *Ibid.,* pp. 64–65.

3. Charles C. Jones, *Religious Instruction of the Negroes. An Address Delivered before the General Assembly of the Presbyterian Church at Augusta, Ga., December 10, 1861* (Richmond, Va.: Presbyterian Committee of Publication, n. d.), p. 24.

4. Catoe Jones to Charles Jones, September 3, 1852, JCTU; also found in *Blacks in Bondage,* pp. 47–50.

5. Charles Jones to Cato Jones, January 28, 1851; also found in *Blacks in Bondage,* p. 44; *ibid.,* pp. 53–55, 47.

6. *RINUS,* p. 110; Myers, *Children of Pride,* p. 929.

7. Genovese, *Roll, Jordan, Roll,* p. 97; Myers, *Children of Pride,* pp. 1304, 1241, 185–186, 1310.

8. Stacy, *Midway Church,* pp. 185–89.

9. Daniel Alexander Payne, *Recollections of Seventy Years* (New York: Arno Press and The New York Times, 1968), pp. 162, 35–37.

10. *Ibid.,* pp. 15–17, 34–35, 162–163.

11. Lilly, *Historic Churches of Charleston,* pp. 156–57; Smyth, *Autobiographical Notes,* p. 206.

12. Lilly, *Historic Churches of Charleston,* pp. 124–25; 2–3, 122–23, 42–43, 46–47; Smyth, *Autobiographical Notes,* pp. 694–96.

13. Adger, *My Life and Times,* pp. 176–77; Lilly, *Historic Churches of Charleston,* pp. 154–55.

14. Payne, *Recollections,* p. 163; Lilly, *Historic Churches of Charleston,* pp. 52–53.

15. Payne, *Recollections,* pp. 162–63, 36–39.

INDEX

177, 180; black members leave to form new church, 177–78
class leaders, 152, 165–67. See also *black leaders*
classes for blacks, in Charleston, 117–19, 126–27, 152, 166; in Liberty County, 25, 43–49, 51–52, 165
Clay, Thomas, 102
clothes for slaves, 71, 73–74, 80, 134
Colonel's Island, 10
Columbia Theological Seminary, 65, 172, 178
communion services, slave participation in Charleston churches, 133–34
Cordoza, F.L., 177
Corker, Joe, 97
Cruckshank, Amos, 125, 127
Cumberland Methodist Church. See *Methodist Churches of Charleston*
Cumming, Susan, 80, 174

-D-
Dahomey, 8
Dent, Francis, 92, 97, 138, 140
DeReef, Joseph, 92
DeReef, Richard, 92
DeReef family, 136
DeSaussure family, 86
Dorchester, S.C., 16
Douglass, Frederick, 18, 142–43
Drayton, Boston, 125
Drayton, Grimké, 101
Drayton, Henry, 125, 127
Dunumn, Adam, 169
Dunwoody, John, 21, 54

-E-
education of blacks, 119–21. See also *classes for blacks*
Elliott, John, 21
Elliott, Stephen, xiii, 142
Elmore, Francis H., 145
Emmanuel African Methodist Episcopal Church, 124–28, 130, 146, 179
England, John, xiii, 90, 116
Episcopal Churches of Charleston, 87–88, 101; and a separate church for blacks, 147–49; and slave baptisms,

132–33; and slave marriages, 134–35, 156–57; Calvary, 137, 149–50; St. Michael's, 87, 116, 137, 147–48; St. Peter's, 101, 137; St. Philip's, 88, 116, 136, 148
"Euphrat Society," 122
Evangelical Alliance, 143
Evans, Martha, 92

-F-
First (Scots) Presbyterian Church. See *Presbyterian Churches of Charleston*
food for slaves, 43, 71
Forrest, John, 88
Forsyth, John, 116
Fraser's Plantation, 30
Frazier, E. Franklin, 165
free blacks, xiii–xiv, 92–93, 109, 125–28, 136–37
Free Church of Scotland and "blood stained money from Charleston," 141–44
Frelinghuysen, Theodore, 24
French Huguenot Church, 88
frizzled chickens, 42. See also *witchcraft*
Frost, Thomas, 136
Fuller, Richard, xiii, 101, 147
funeral services of slaves, 32–33, 136–39
funeral societies, 136–38

-G-
Gadsden, Bishop, xiii
gardens for slaves, 73
Garrison, William Lloyd, 142
Genovese, Eugene, 174
Gettysbury Lutheran Seminary, 128
Gildersleeve, Benjamin, 102
Gilman, Samuel, 88
Girardeau, John L., xiii, 151–53, 164, 178
Grimké, Angelina, 101, 102
Grimké, Sara, 101, 102
Grimké, Thomas Drayton, 101, 102
grog shops, 98
Gullah dialect, 151
Gullah Jack, 147
Gurley, R. R., 24